AF407518

CASTRO'S DRUG CARTEL

Copyright © 2022 Pablo Padula, Lazaro Garcia Fonseca
All rights reserved. No part of this publication may be reproduced, distributed, or transmitted in any form or by any means, including photocopying, recording, or other electronic or mechanical methods, without the prior written permission of the publisher, except in the case of brief quotations embodied in critical reviews and certain other noncommercial uses permitted by copyright law. For permission requests, write to the publisher, addressed "Attention: Permissions Coordinator," at the address below.
This book is based on a true story. Some of the dialogs and situations that appear on the book have been recreated based on historical data and some are products of the author's imagination.
Front cover image by Cristobal Herrera
Book design by Pablo Padula
First printing edition 2022

FOREWORD

Much has been said during the last 5 decades about the participation of Fidel Castro and his brother Raul in drug trafficking. Hundreds of books and even famous television series such as "Narcos", on Netflix, link the man who said he hated drugs with all his soul to the smuggling of thousands of tons of drugs into the United States.

What had never been proven before, with so much irrefutable evidence, is that the Cuban government actively participated, and with malice, in the creation of the famous golden age of drug trafficking in Miami, the 1980s. Nor was it known, until now, that the Castros sent hundreds of undercover agents to the Florida coast during the famous "Mariel Exodus", whose purpose was to create an organization of drug traffickers willing to flood the country with drugs from Colombia and thus destroy the United States from inside.

If someone refuses to believe this truth, it is because they do not know the Castros or the history that exists between the two countries. In addition to the well-known scandal that featured the famous anti-Castro group Brothers to the Rescue, where Cuban agents infiltrated to destroy it from within, the very CIA stationed undercover agents on the island during the missile crisis in 1962. Historically, the United States and Cuba have exchanged spies more often than diplomatic contacts. It would be highly innocent to believe that the Cuban government did not take advantage of the situation created by the massive exodus of Cubans that left the port of Mariel in 1980 to send its undercover men, posing as victims when in reality they were the perpetrators.

In 1982, US authorities arrested and prosecuted Cuban Mario Estévez González, the captain of the Lazy Lady ship, used to transport drugs from Cuba to Florida. He testified at his trial that he was a Cuban government agent first sent to the United States in 1980 during the Mariel boatlift for the purpose of infiltrating the Miami anti-Castro group known as Alpha 66. He also later testified that he was instructed by his superiors in the Cuban Ministry of the Interior to infiltrate drug traffickers in the Bahamas and learn how to buy and sell drugs in the United States.

The officer in charge of communicating with Estevez told him that "it is important for us to fill the United States with drugs." He also ordered her to go to Bimini in the Bahamas in late September or early October 1980 to meet with the Cuban government agent known as Frank Bonilla, the owner of the Lazy Lady, and help with a stalled drug shipment in Cuba. Estévez also stated that he, Bonilla and Pérez met with René Rodríguez, the Cuban president of ICAP, and with Aldo Santamaria Cuadrado, Vice Admiral of the Cuban Navy, two high-ranking officials of the Castro government who guarded the 10 million quaalude tablets in the mothership, the Viviana. Estévez testified that Santamaría, the Vice Admiral of the Cuban Navy, introduced himself as René Baeza Rodríguez and joked about Estevez's drug smuggling. He touched me, put his hand on me and said: 'Finally you're going to have a pharmacy in Miami.' Estevez also testified that, following the orders of his Cuban government control officers, he smuggled cocaine into the United States and took more than $2 million in proceeds from the cocaine trade back to Cuba.

He also revealed during his interrogation that there were marijuana plantations on the island in the Manzanillo and Escambray areas, all operated and supervised by the Cuban General Directorate of Intelligence.

Estévez is one of the many undercover agents of the Castro regime who participated in drug trafficking activities representing the government of Fidel Castro. It is believed that more than 7,000 Cuban spies reached US shores during the Mariel boatlift.

The rest of the immigrants came to the United States at a very special time in history. Tons of drugs were anxiously waiting to reach their destination, the country where there was enough money to make traffickers millionaires. And the profits were fabulous.

Whoever saw the movie "Scarface" knows perfectly well what was happening in Miami since the end of the 70's, the city had become a paradise for Colombian and Cuban drug traffickers. Tony Montana may have been a fantasy character and some of his scenes, like the one with his death, exaggerated for dramatic purposes, but fiction isn't much better than truth. The life of the character played by Al Pacino was quite similar to that of many Cubans who arrived in the United States without a peso and great aspirations, after decades of repression, hunger and false expectations. Except for the violence and explicit language, the stories from that time are a lot like hundreds of Marielitos that came to "the Yuma" as they call it in Cuba, in search of a better life.

In the film, Tony is a Cuban immigrant who realizes that in Miami it is possible to make easy money dealing drugs and killing people. The earnings, without a doubt, far exceed the minimum wage that he could achieve working in a factory. In a short time Montana transforms his life completely, reaching the level of drug lord.

It is also rumored that many of the fortunes of Cuban immigrants who opened successful businesses in Miami originated in drug trafficking.

- Anyone who had a boat at that time could win fortunes in those days - says Yoel, one of the protagonists of this book. He then mentioned names and companies of very prominent people in the Cuban community in Florida that I would not dare to reveal without proof. I'll take the secret to the grave.

During his last 10 years in prison, the main character of this book, Lazaro Garcia Fonseca, had the opportunity to talk with one of those Cuban spies, who told him how the MC, an army unit dependent on the Ministry of the Interior that we will talk about extensively later, he coordinated drug trafficking operations between the coasts of both countries, facilitating the movement of tons of marijuana and cocaine into the United States. All this was done with the full knowledge of the highest leadership of the communist party, as was customary on the island: "not a fly flew in Cuba without the explicit consent of Fidel," according to popular jargon.

This book is called "El Cartel de los Castro" because we have proven, with irrefutable evidence, that these two are the leaders of a secret group of criminals sent to the United States with the purpose of participating in drug trafficking activities. They did it for their own financial gain and also because they believed that drugs would do what they never could: destroy a society they hated so much.

In this diagram we show, in a simplified way, how this criminal cartel operates:

CASTRO'S CARTEL STRUCTURE

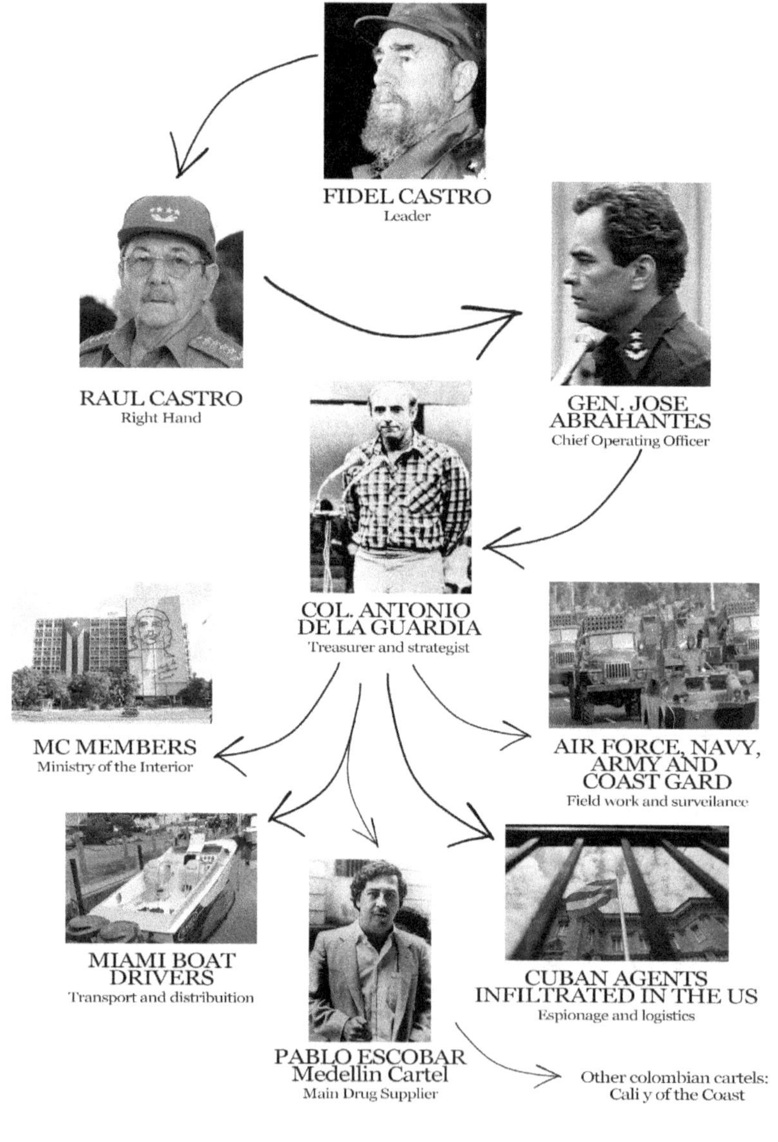

A drug cartel not only refers to the drugs that are trafficked but also to the people who make it up. A cartel has hierarchies, links, rules, risks, consequences and, above all, motivations. And in this book we are going to propose a hypothesis that may surprise many, but that will undoubtedly make them think. Were the Castros responsible for the fact that people like Lazaro or Yoel, whom you will meet later, have dedicated themselves to drug trafficking?

Let's use another famous example. The story of Salvador Magluta and Willy Falcon. The "Cocaine Cowboys" were the main characters in the Miami news headlines and also in a Netflix series. They managed to smuggle 75 tons of cocaine into the United States, earning them more than $2 billion in profits.

What do Magluta and Falcón have to do with the story of this book? That they are both Cubans and that most of the members of their organization, their "Cartel", were also people born in Cuba, determined to risk their lives and freedom in exchange for amounts of money impossible to obtain by other means.

As you read this story you will realize that there is an evident and very strong pattern between them and Lazaro Garcia Fonseca, whose family also admired his work as a drug trafficker and never opposed it. All his accomplices, those who decided to keep quiet and cover them up and many others who decided to take that risky path to achieve the American dream, were Cubans.

Fidel Castro and his false revolution have not only been responsible for an unimaginable level of misery and a massive immigration of compatriots, but also created the reasons for thousands of Cubans to travel the 90 miles that separate the two countries and seek their fortunes. , at the risk of ending up dead or in jail. "The end justifies the means", they think, with good reason.

The way Lazaro tells his story will allow the reader to fully understand this phenomenon.

Colombians were the forerunners of drug trafficking, there is no doubt about that, driven by an internal armed conflict that began in the 1960s and needed financing; and by the global demand for drugs that increased considerably in the 1970s, especially in the United States. All this gave rise to the famous Medellín and Cali cartels, the main ones, and then many others that began to emerge in Colombia and Mexico, the southern neighbor with enviable access to 'gringolandia'.

Since the 1970s, Cuba has been a highly coveted springboard for Colombian drug cartels. A speedboat driven by a good pilot could bring hundreds of kilos of drugs to North American shores in a matter of minutes. The Bahamas were, and still are, also another point widely used by the mbianos to enter narcotics into Florida. Lazaro used both routes to move the drug.

It will never be known if the supposed hatred that Fidel Castro always manifested against narcotics was real or a simple façade to show himself magnanimous and show off his leadership. Remember that he is the same man who said in 1959: "Regarding Communism, I can only tell you one thing, I am not a communist, nor do communists have the strength to be a determining factor in my country... This revolution is not communist but humanist", he lied blatantly during a speech at the American Society of Newspaper Editors in Washington DC.

Depending on whom you ask, Castro changed a lot over the years, and what he once thought may have become a mask he wore to hide his insatiable lust for power. In other words, maybe he hated drugs and the consequences they left on society, but when he needed to generate money to keep his political circus afloat (and in the process hurt Yuma), everything was allowed.

Lazaro himself says that Castro stopped being the same as he was leading towards the abyss of others, that his speech stopped being about ideas and became about mental control and appearances. That is why much of the new information that you will read in this book fits perfectly with the times that were lived then. For example, the famous "MC" of the Ministry of the Interior, created to circumvent the embargo. Human, drug, and technology smuggling, all under the same pretext, to alleviate the enormous economic burden left to Cuba by the fall of the Soviet Union.

Writing this introduction, Netflix's Korean series "Squid Game" comes to mind, which had great audience success, among other things, because it raises an existential question that many ask: what would a human being be willing to do to reach his goals. Die, let others die, kill, if necessary? If any reader did not see it, the plot is about a man full of debts and family problems who is offered the option of earning many millions of won, the Korean currency. After accepting, the protagonist realizes that to receive the money many other people have to die, including family and friends. I recommend that you see it, and that's why I'm not going to tell you anything else. I just leave you this information.

Did Fidel Castro and his revolution full of political and social hypocrisy, with its cruel and oppressive tactics, create an ambitious and repressed people, willing to do whatever it takes to achieve their dreams, including risking their lives and freedom?

But the biggest question is this: did the Castros know that by allowing thousands of people out of Mariel they were essentially handing over labor to the drug cartels that were already operating in 1980? Worse still: did they do it on purpose to cause the United States a double blow: create an immigration crisis and provide an army of potential drug traffickers?

This book was written under these premises, so that the whole world can analyze the impact that the presence of a totalitarian regime has had just 90 miles from the most powerful country in the world, determined to destroy its nemesis at any cost.

After all, it was Fidel Castro who said: 'Drugs can do more damage to imperialism than atomic bombs'

In this book we will tell the story of 2 Marielitos who were murdered for allegedly stealing a huge sum of money from a mafia boss. Beyond the perpetrator of the crime, they were killed by poverty, ambition and the lack of perspective to survive in this country. His tragedy is just one example of the corruption that money exerts on people, especially those who come from a regime where world reality is completely unknown.

Lazaro always tells me: "you are almost as smart as me". At first my reaction was to think that a person who spent almost 2 decades of his life in prison is not exactly the king of intelligence. But then, as I got to know his story, my reasoning radically changed. Now I say: who is more intelligent, a poor journalist who struggles every day to support his children, with tight money and large debts in the future, or a brave man, almost without scruples, who amassed an enormous fortune, paid for his children's studies, bought them all houses and, as a consequence, spent 13 years in jail?

I leave that question to the readers so that, once this book is finished, they can answer it on social networks.

WHO IS LAZARO GARCIA FONSECA?

"And it is that in the treacherous world, there is nothing true or false: everything is according to the color of the glass with which it is seen."
Ramon de Campoamor y Campoosorio (1817-1901)

Before meeting him, many might think that Lazaro Felipe Garcia Fonseca is an ex-convict who decided to dedicate to a life of crime to satisfy his basic instincts. That is the concept that society usually has about all those who are dedicated to smuggling and transporting drugs. At the end of this book, it is likely that many of you will realize that this is a premise as wrong as it is premature.

It can be assumed, with certainty, that human beings are the product of the society that raises us, that we do not always make decisions based on individual intelligence but rather as a reaction to the reality that saw us grow up. And Lazaro is a product of communism, and there is no doubt about that.

Communism has many facets: one, that it is a failed and proven obsolete system, which works only for those in power. Another, that turns people into beings lost in time, incapable of evaluating their lives objectively. It isolates them from the rest of the world, condemns them to backwardness.

Lazaro is one of those facets. A man who was never satisfied with the fate that others painted for him, who immediately realized when the revolution triumphed that this was a terrible idea. For this reason, at the age of 14, they put him in jail, with 3 shots in his body.

- I say repudiation, not revolution, repudiation, because everything he does rots. Like, for example, he made the Cuban family disunite. Some took the path of the most faithful, like 95%, and others went against Fidel, 5%. At the time when everyone said: Fidel or Death, I had other ideas.

- Were you against your dad? - I asked, surprised.

- Yes, my dad was a Fidelista, they got sick with Fidel. 3 of my brothers too. My family was destroyed because of the revolution. Several of my cousins were shot for opposing.

His disillusionment with Castro's ideas began the day the new government took from his father a bus that his uncle had given her.

-I couldn't be happy with that, because apart from confiscating our livelihood, apart from losing the mechanic shop and losing the buses, my uncle lost his family, because my father had joined the militia and his three children too. .

Lazaro joined the resistance, but passively, helping his uncle.

- I had already taken sides with those who were against it. And once in Sierra del Rosario, Pinar del Río, when I was taking medicine to my cousin, Castro's troops shot me 3 times, scars that I still have on my body. I am reminded of my adolescence every day.

Lazaro miraculously survived. A government nurse picked him up in a helicopter and rushed him to a hospital where his life was saved.

- Fidel transformed the minds of Cubans. Fidel made him not believe in God. He made them renounce their faith. He hypnotized them with promises. That happens a lot in the towns, Germany, for example. Why did Germany support Hitler so much even though he caused millions of deaths? And why in Russia did they support Lenin? Both knew how to take advantage of a historical moment full of weakness and uncertainty and used that support and fanaticism to brainwash the people. But he couldn't wash it for me. God did not want me to wash it off and when they shot me and put me in jail, my mind changed forever, I only thought of having a bright future, far from that madness. - explains Lazaro wistfully.

It is not unreasonable to think that some of Fidel Castro's ideas remained impregnated in Lazaro's mind. It is impossible to believe that the constant barrage of revolutionary ideas completely slipped through the mind of an impressionable young man, whom his family considered brilliant.

- I think I'm very intelligent. I think I am an intelligent person. I would never have agreed with the revolution, however there were professors, doctors and university professors who became fanatics of the Revolution. - Lázaro says with certainty. - And it is that Fidel knew how to use the hatred that Latin America has for the United States, because in the United States they have also made mistakes, they invaded Panama and took it away from Colombia. They have invaded Mexico many times, they took half of Mexico from the Mexicans and that is not a good thing. I remember an episode when a US sailor urinated on top of the Martí statue in Havana's Central Park. The communists always knew how to exploit these facts. -

The question that this book poses is: What role did that legitimate resentment expressed by Castro and many leaders and inhabitants of the Americas play in the decisions of people like Lazaro, who dedicated themselves to drug trafficking knowing perfectly well the social consequences of drug use? Could the anti-Yankee rhetoric have had weight at the moment of dedicating his life to the dangerous but generous business of drug trafficking?

Didn't you feel guilty knowing you were dealing drugs? - asked.

- That I was carrying marijuana? No, it's almost legal now. - He replied, a little shaken. - Now it is medicinal. The truth is that at that time I had a family to support and that turned out to be my only alternative. I tried to start a house painting business but it was not enough for me at all. I wanted to study English but they didn't give me the schedules. So this opportunity to move drugs came along and I took it. Many Cubans were doing it at that time, the early 1980s. It was fast money and a lot of it, but it wasn't easy at all.

- Sure, you earned money, but you ran the risk of being killed or imprisoned. - The most logical question came out of my mouth at that moment.

- Listen to me, you have to understand. There is a psychiatrist or psychologist named Sigmund Freud. He says that there are four giants of human feeling. Do you know which one is the first? The sense of duty. I felt the duty to give my family a good life, that was what always motivated me.

- Have you ever felt remorse? -

- None, none, I have never felt remorse for what I have done. I know I did bad things, but hey: they say that he who sins and prays, ties.

In our talk, Lazaro told me a story that clearly demonstrates his way of thinking and living:

-A man is going to say goodbye to his son at the airport and tells him:-"You are going to live in another country, to find your destiny. I give you this wise advice: "Earn your money honestly." - "And if I can't? - the son replies. Then his father looks him straight in the eye and says, "So, earn your money."

Lazaro sat up a little in the chair and continued to reflect on his life.

- I remember that once I returned home frustrated because an operation fell through and my wife told me when she saw my face: "Didn't you do anything?" "I didn't do anything," I replied. And she told me: "if this continues, I think you're going to have to go back to painting". I got a big laugh. "No, mommy, everything will be fine, believe me. Nobody is going to look for help in my house, you will never need anything, I promise you. If I can't crown a trip, another will come. Because now I either carry marijuana or I die, because now it is a personal thing, it is no longer a business."

Another reason for the boom in drug trafficking between Cuba and the United States, in addition to Colombian supply and Yankee demand, was the fact that hundreds of Cuban boatmen lost their jobs in the late 1970s when lobster fishing was suspended in the Cuban coasts. All that unemployed workforce was quickly taken advantage of by drug traffickers, who paid exorbitant amounts for each load that reached the Florida coast.

Lazaro didn't know much about boats, charters, or drug smuggling, but he learned quickly.

In the beginning, nothing was easy. He had to wait several weeks before getting his first big payday. Sometimes the plane crashed, didn't take off, or the cargo didn't arrive for various reasons. But once he got the hang of the business and connected with the right people, the wads of cash started pouring in. With his earnings, which could reach hundreds of thousands of dollars in a day, he bought boats and from then on, that was his full-time job.

Paradoxically, his journey into the world of drugs had begun, years ago, also on a boat.

After years of trying to escape his fate as an anti-Castro, Lazaro broke out of a jail in Cuba and boarded a ship bound for Miami. But he did not run away like many others, he was part of a movement called "El Mariel" invented by Fidel Castro to punish the United States with a human invasion. In total, more than 125,000 Cubans left the country through Port Mariel between April and December 1980, receiving, for this reason, the pseudonym "marielitos".

As part of his Machiavellian plan and to try to hide the fact that people were leaving because Cuba was a country with no future or present, Castro announced that the "marielitos" were all criminals, undesirables who were being expelled from the country. His purpose was to discredit the "traitors" who left the country and create problems for them wherever they went, in addition to giving the gringos the feeling that their country was being invaded by criminals, murderers and predators.

Although there were problems with many of these Cuban immigrants, in reality, time has shown that none of this was true, but rather an unfortunate political strategy of a man who hated the United States with all his soul. The "marielitos" are now the foundation of a huge and thriving community that put down very fruitful roots in South Florida, not only economically but also culturally powerful.

The immediate effect of this enormous exodus was the migratory crisis it caused in the United States, from the time they arrived at the port of Key West until their immersion in Miami society. There were hundreds of thousands of people who needed food, lodging and a relatively certain future.

Between all of them there was Lazaro, with his wife, Dr. Merida Garcia and their 3 children: Gisselle, Carlos and Yanet. 4 human beings on his back, without work or place to live. Luckily, an aunt, Aida Fonseca, welcomed them into her home.

Very soon Lazaro realized that the price of freedom in "Yuma" was going to be very high and his pride, sense of duty and morality would face many conflicts. Luckily, he was very clear about what he was willing to do to achieve his goals.

Luckily?

His career as a "merchandise transporter", as he describes himself, took him to travel thousands of kilometers on 3 continents, earn several million dollars but also spend just under 15 years in jail.

I invite you to read the rest of the book to judge, with arguments, if it was luck or not.

CHAPTER 0

THE SCAPE-GOAT

When the door of the dark cell opened, the prisoner realized that he had only a few moments to live.

On the horizon, the sun barely painted some timid oranges. It was the early morning of July 13, 1989 and there was a smell of betrayal in the air.

- What's this? I demand to speak with the commander-he managed to say with a broken voice, full of panic. - Do not approach me, soldier, I order you, I am a general of the Cuban Revolution.

The words of the decorated hero of Angola fell on deaf ears. The men in green uniforms took the burly prisoner by the arms, put the handcuffs on him in front of him and dragged him out of the cell.

Ochoa, while walking slowly and shaking, kept screaming.

-Let me talk to Fidel, I'm sure he will listen to me. -In the voice of the soldier there was an unrestrained cry that was not in keeping with his famous brave and confident attitude.

For the first time in his life, the man who risked everything for an ideal, who fought for several decades to defend the name of his country and his leader, felt a deep hatred for Fidel Castro. His former great friend, the same one who had promised him never to come to that moment, to take his life, was carrying out the most horrible betrayal.

Every step down the long, dark hallway hurt like a knife. Former General Arnaldo Ochoa Sanchez's mind could not process what was happening as he tried to shout orders to a group of men who would no longer listen to him.

Outside the prison, a military truck was waiting with the engine running. They put him in with a guard on each side and immediately the vehicle started in a hurry.

No one wanted that moment to last longer than necessary.

Ochoa tried once again to convince the military, who previously swore the highest respect to him, to help save his life.

-Delgado, I know his family. You introduced me to his wife and children at a Revolution anniversary celebration last year, he said looking for sympathy.

Captain Delgado, who was at the wheel, had completely forgotten about that event and felt even more remorse. But he sank deeper into his silence. He was following orders from the Commander of him, and those were holy words.

When they arrived at the place designated to carry out the sentence, Ochoa realized that there was no turning back.

In a small cell, next to the entrance, he recognized his colleagues Antonio de la Guardia, Army Colonel, Major Amado Padron, his right-hand man for many years, and Captain Jorge Martinez, Ochoa's assistant and the man accused of having met with Pablo Escobar himself.

They 4, along with 10 others involved, were the protagonists of one of the most famous trials in Cuban history. They had been accused, among other crimes, of smuggling more than 6 tons of Colombian cocaine into the United States, taking advantage of Cuba's military structure and its proximity to the Florida coast. The loot: 3.4 million dollars, money that was never recovered, simply because all the profits from drug trafficking were controlled and distributed by the Castro brothers themselves.

Ochoa defended himself mildly during the trial, which was uncharacteristic of his battle-hardened and courageous personality. He said he was unaware of the activities of De la Guardia and the other defendants in relation to drug trafficking. The judicial process, broadcast on television, something extremely rare in the Castro era, was minutely controlled by the supreme commander, who was hidden behind a one-way mirror. The decorated general knew that any brave or spontaneous confession involving the country's high command could cost him and his entire family his life.

In the end, Ochoa admitted his guilt and resigned himself to the possibility of being shot for his crimes. The same process was experienced by the 3 men who were now very close to him waiting for the same fate. The rest of the defendants were given different sentences. One of them was the twin brother of Colonel de la Guardia, Patricio, who received a 30-year sentence.

Historians and witnesses of this aberrant and sad page of Cuban history say that Fidel Castro was very envious and afraid of losing power in the hands of a more admirable and better prepared man such as General Ochoa. Since he returned in triumph from Angola, he had become a stone in the shoe of the revered Caribbean leader.

This is how Norberto Fuentes describes that moment in history in his book "Drug Trafficking and Revolutionary Tasks":

"Now we know that, during that period, Fidel Castro commissioned repeated surveys through the so-called States of Opinion, which is his means of feeling Cuban public opinion, to see the reaction of the people to this campaign to destroy one of the most prestigious and popular officers who had emerged from the revolution.

The first poll surprised and scared Fidel Castro, with 98 percent expressing sympathy for Ochoa. This convinced him of the imperative need for the incident to end with his execution. The execution was not carried out until support for Ochoa had dropped sufficiently, although, even so, Fidel had to admit when confirming the death sentence that the polls revealed that the Cuban people did not approve of such a severe sanction.

It was possible to speculate that, in some way, General Ochoa was involved in a conspiracy with the Soviets. The passivity of the Soviets in the face of the execution of one of their best allies within the Cuban military hierarchy was surprising, whether or not he had been conspiring with them. On one occasion, after the USSR had disintegrated, Mr. Pavlov, who had been the Soviet Undersecretary of Foreign Affairs for Latin America at the time, answered evasively when I asked him that question. This hypothesis was based somewhat on the analogy of that possibility with the accusation made by Eric Honecker, the leader of East Germany, that General Secretary Gorbachev had promoted the downfall of Ceausescu in Romania by encouraging a military conspiracy through the GRU, the Soviet military intelligence agency.

This hypothesis was also based on the version that had reached Radio Martí at that time that General Ochoa was in the initial stages of obtaining information about the drugs to justify a military coup against Fidel before Cuban public opinion. "

A very dangerous combination for the Castros: Ochoa was a sympathizer of perestroika and, to top it off, he had great influence among the island's military. There were already plenty of reasons to eliminate it. But he couldn't get it out of the way alone, Fidel Castro had to create a much broader criminal network to justify such a purge. That is why the defendants were 14 and not just one.

What was also known through stories collected from the networks, is that Cuban spies working for the Castro brothers were able to record private conversations between Ochoa, De la Guardia, Padron and Martinez where they were heard saying that the Cuban leader was no longer useful. to do his job and that it was time to get him out of the way.

That is an absolute truth. Iliana de la Guardia, Antonio's daughter and Patricio's niece, once told the press: "Ochoa didn't keep quiet about anything. In front of me one day, at Patricio's house, she said, this has to change, it can't go on like this, this man is crazy, what are we going to do with the crazy one.

All these signs of change, which were also taking place in the Soviet Union, added to the fact that the US government had opened a formal investigation to find out the level of participation of the Cuban government in drug trafficking, were sufficient reasons to carry out a trial so summary that from the beginning of the process to the execution of the condemned, hardly a month passed.

There are theories that Ochoa was in the process of creating his own links with Pablo Escobar, because he thought about the possibility of establishing a cocaine processing plant in Angola. He wanted to take advantage of the distribution networks established by Colonel Tony de la Guardia to traffic drugs to the United States and Europe. Taking into account that De la Guardia was in charge of organizing all drug trafficking operations for the Castro brothers, it was assumed that Ochoa's plans were approved by the cartel bosses. However, this plan was never carried out and, therefore, it is only a rumor that is going around the internet.

This raises another question: was it perhaps Pablo Escobar who sent word to Fidel that General Ochoa was trying to negotiate with him behind his back? Could that have been another factor that sealed the sad fate of Angola's decorated hero?

In short, eliminating Ochoa and De la Guardia, two of his most "dear" collaborators and friends, was, in the twisted mind of Fidel Castro, the only way to clean up his image and retain power in a political moment that was changing rapidly and dangerously before his very eyes. It was "the ultimate sacrifice" to proclaim his innocence to the world.

The firing squad moved into position. They were 5 mid-rank officers who volunteered to carry out the mission. They were offered no reward, only the perverse satisfaction of doing something good for the revolution, to please the commander. In their hands they had Russian rifles with bullets personally approved by Fidel Castro.

General Ochoa would have said at some point after his trial that he would have the face of his former friend in his mind when they put him in front of the wall. One can only speculate what he thought, but the bullets penetrated his body and the darkness came at last.

Witnesses say that the officer in charge of the execution approached to give him a coup de grâce in the head. It is not known if this is a common practice of Cuban justice or if this was the posthumous message from Fidel Castro.

The only thing certain is that General Arnaldo Ochoa did not deserve such an end.

Once a group of soldiers removed Ochoa's lifeless body, the other prisoners followed. One by one they faced the firing squad that ended their lives, extinguished by a whim of power that history will always judge cruel and unnecessary. Only to the mind of a sadistic dictator, who lived and died stained with the blood of his people, was this atrocity justified.

His 4 fatal victims and all the others sentenced to prison fell into an ideological trap with no way out. Disobeying the Castro brothers was impossible, all they did was follow orders, as a good military man always does. In the same way that those 5 soldiers pulled the trigger and witnessed how 4 lives were extinguished forever, Ochoa, De la Guardia, Martinez and Padron carried out orders from a superior.

Cuban history is full of examples of imprisonment or death for disobedience. It is a country where, for the last 60 years, saying a single word against the regime is equivalent to an absurd conviction without trial or defense counsel. In Cuba being a political prisoner or for ideological reasons is easier than getting soap to wash clothes.

Nothing happens in Cuba without the knowledge of the heads of the Castro Cartel, much less the passage of 6 tons of cocaine, or the hundreds of thousands of tons that passed before and after. In a country that is characterized by having one of the most complex networks of internal espionage, which allowed the people to always be in a panic of being put in jail for speaking ill of the government, it is impossible to think that hundreds of planes coming from Colombia They passed through there without reaching the ears of the highest leadership of the government.

Besides, what would an army general do with millions of dollars in his possession? Travel to Europe and buy expensive cars? That is simply absurd in a country whose poverty levels are internationally famous.

The same thing happened a short time later during the trial of the Minister of the Interior General Jose Abrahantes. Among the many accusations brought against him was that he made unauthorized purchases of new vehicles for personnel under his command. Who believes that it is possible to make such an expense without it reaching the ears of Fidel or his brother?

No one.

CHAPTER 1

THE ARREST ON THE HIGH SEA

It was one of those nights where everything that could go wrong was going wrong. Lazaro, Manolo, Juan Carlos and Yoel had spent the entire day on the high seas pretending to fish, because they had been late the night before. It was dawn and it was very dangerous to go to the Keys passing in front of the city of Miami in a suspicious boat. Due to the plane taking too long to reach the drop off point, they were forced to wait until dark.

They floated for 12 hours, exposed, in the open air, with 2,000 kilos of marijuana in the hold.

Ten o'clock arrived at night and it did not stop raining, but they still decided that it was the best time to do the operation. They passed between a mass of concrete cast into stone, something known as the sunken ship and Cat Key, they entered the channel that divides the Bahama Bank and the Florida Peninsula, under a heavy downpour that made them navigate almost blindly. The cold water droplets felt like stones hitting their faces.

- This is not normal, as soon as I get to Miami I'm going to see my godfather so he can do a cleanse - Yoel told him.

- I'm not superstitious, but I'm about to believe in the curse of the old sailor - Lázaro replied.

After more than 3 hours of navigation, lost not on course, but in the distance, and completely blinded by the rain, they suddenly felt something incredible that froze them, because the boat had suddenly stopped.

A dry blow. The boat stopped violently. The silence of the night was broken by Yoel's anguished voice.

"We're stuck in a sand bank and mud," he said, with a frightened face as he leaned overboard with a matchbox in his hand, which immediately went out every time he lit it.

Lazaro was always the calmest of the group, the one who injected sanity into the others. But tonight the mishaps and the rain had transformed him into a very different version of himself.

- I shit on your mother's pussy, zingado boat! He yelled with all his might.

They could not believe what they were experiencing. It was like a nightmare, a bad dream, but unfortunately it was real.

- We're nailed to a bass - Yoel said again.

Lazaro looked at him, recovered his calm a bit and said:

-The issue is to know where we are, I was sure that we were sailing in the open sea-he answered looking around him, in search of some light or reflection that would locate him.

Remember that at that time, 1985, there was no GPS.

Yoel immediately realized that the course error they had made could have been catastrophic, that they were miraculously alive.

"Luckily it wasn't a stone," he said with some shyness, understanding what his words implied.

The truth is that they were about to collide with a stone and if that impact had occurred, at the speed that they were sailing, which was about 50 miles per hour, they would have been shattered.

Without going any further, many will remember the tragic death of Jose Fermandez, the 24-year-old Marlins pitcher, who crashed into some stones off the coast of Miami Beach on September 25, 2016. That is what could have happened to him. having passed Lazaro and Yoel that night, almost 3 decades ago.

He stopped raining as if by magic and the night cleared up completely. The question they asked themselves was answered by their sight, because soon they could see that they had run aground in the middle of Biscayne Bay, in front of the city of Miami, with all its splendor and beauty, with its great buildings right under their noses. . They stood with their mouths open.

- Look where we came to run aground with 4000 pounds in the crop, not even the Chinese doctor will save us from this

- said Yoel and added - Well, gentlemen, we must fight for life, death is certain. -

- And what can we do now? Manolo asked Lázaro that as captain he had to make a decision quickly.

- The only solution that I see is to throw everything we bring into the water to lighten the weight of the boat and get it out of here - Lázaro replied.

- But the current is going to drag everything - interrupted Juan Carlos.

- No, if we tie it with the anchor rope - answered Yoel.

- By removing weight from the boat it will float again - Lazaro continued - there are only 80 packages, so if we don't start quickly this work will be eternal. -

"But that's going to be a titan effort," Juan Carlos pointed out, frightened.

- Have no doubts about that, and we have to do it before dawn, remember the peasant saying that "loaded donkey looks for a path", so get to work kids - Yoel ordered them.

- The light of day is going to give us away, now is when we have to show who we are, the battle is lost when one gives up and we don't know how to give up.

Manolo finished Lázaro's idea by saying:

- The best do not give up, nor do they ever retire.-

They took out the packages and threw them into the water tied with the anchor rope, one by one. With everything in the water, Manolo and Juan Carlos held the cape against the current.

By physical rule, the boat, without 4,400 pounds of weight, 4,000 of merchandise and 400 of the weight of Manolo and Juan Carlos, floated again. They placed it in the channel, and as they said, it was a titan's job to get the packages back up. They no longer weighed 50 pounds each, now they were 70, adding the sea water that entered the packages due to the time they were submerged.

When they finished, the star king had risen from the east, forming a beautiful aurora for everyone, except for them.

- And what are we going to do now? Because it's already dawn, said Juan Carlos, the youngest of all, who despite his lack of experience maintained his poise at all times.

The sun continued to give its morning show, poking its head over the line of the horizon delivering another beautiful sunrise, a unique spectacle worth enjoying, in other more favorable circumstances.

-Look what a beautiful sunrise, how right Marti was when she said in one of her poems that the count had his ancestry and the dawn had the beggar, said Lázaro trying to hide his physical and mental exhaustion.

- No, please, no, not poetry now, the oven isn't for cookies or butter for pork rinds - Yoel said.

Manolo took the floor to ease tensions:

- What can we do? We are never going to change it, I think Lázaro likes history and poetry more than women -

With the speed of lightning, Lázaro answered:

- Nothing about that partner, more than women I don't like anything.

And he added:

- At this time we can no longer enter the mooring hole, we have to do something because in half an hour the fishermen leave and there is always a sneak among them. You can call the Marine Patrol on the radio and things are going to get very ugly, we're going to go out to the canal to kill time until nightfall.

Saying and doing they went out into the channel some 10 or 12 miles away from the coast, within the current of the Gulf of Mexico that runs at a rate of 5 miles, from south to north, to England through the Atlantic Ocean.

- The radar they have in Miami can detect us here - Manolo warned him.

- I know, but there is no other better place, here we have to wait for the night. - Lázaro clarified, making a calming gesture with his hands.

- When it's not your turn, even if you take it off, and when it's your turn, even if you put it on - Yoel sentenced, hearing the silence of the Caribbean Sea, a sea navigated for centuries by pirates and smugglers.

In order not to lose the custom, Lázaro spoke:

- Gentlemen, to break the tension, make yourself comfortable and listen whether you want to or not, and since there is nowhere to run here, you are going to have to listen to a poem by Martín Fierro, by José Hernández, a gaucho poetry that I like very much:

I ask the saints of heaven, to help my thinking,
I ask you at this time, that I will tell my story
Refresh my memory and clarify my understanding
Come miraculous saints, come all to my aid
That my tongue is naked, and my sight is disturbed
I ask God to help me, on this very rough occasion.

- Well, what can we do with poetry at this hour? Manolo asked him.

- Now we can't do anything, but I'm going to put it in my book when I can tell all this incredible adventure - Lázaro replied.

That December 17, 1982 was the day of San Lázaro, a saint highly revered by Cubans, who always believed in him above political ideas, and still continue to venerate him with great faith and hope.

But the hope that that day would be better faded when they realized that the current diverted the boat many miles to the north, to Boca Raton.

The drift was much more than Lázaro had calculated. The day was terrible, but since time did not stop, night came again, a dark and cold night, a night in which the north broke.

In complete darkness, Lázaro ordered Yoel:

- Arrow starts the engines and heads south, we're going to coast to Cayo Largo, it's time to stick to the bull - Yoel obeyed Lázaro's order.

They started sailing at 3,500 turns, 7 miles west of the coast. Again the rain raged with incredible force and they had no choice but to sail blind, the curse of the old sailor had appeared once again with a copious and cold rain. Manolo and Juan Carlos warmed up in the cabin and only Yoel, at the helm, and Lázaro, next to him, remained outside.

"Water above and water below," Yoel yelled at his friend and companion while he held the rudder. Pilot and copilot wet as chickens, dripping with water, already almost resigned to their bad luck.

At that moment, the fairy of fortune that had always accompanied them abandoned them, Lázaro felt a light on the back of his neck. In a split second he realized that his life was about to change forever.

He turned around and saw the 2 Coast Guard boats, approaching quickly, one on each side of their boat.

A gasp came from his throat and he managed to utter a few words:

- Give "leather to the horse", burn the sneakers that are behind us, lower the controls to the table.

- What course do I set? Yoel asked without daring to look.

- Set course east, let's go to the Bahamas, this boat at 70 miles per hour will not stop anyone - said Lázaro.

- Look to the right, another police speed boat is coming, like a bullet headed for us.

From the customs boat using a horn they were told:

- Captain, Captain, we are from the United States Customs Service, stop the boat immediately.

"Ignore him and keep running," Lázaro told him while he yelled at his pursuers: "no spic inglish, no spic inglish".

He suddenly felt like all his fears had come true. The sound of helicopter blades began to be felt above them. Lazaro knew that now there was no escape, if anything could stop them it was that magnificent armed bird.

- We already have the coastguard helicopter on us - Yoel yelled.

"We are from the United States Coast Guard, stop immediately," he heard in the distance from one of the boats that was chasing them.

Yoel had turned to the right looking for the only possible escape: to enter the international waters of the Bahamas. It was not the first time that the authorities persecuted them and the previous times they were able to escape. But unlike today, those times there was no helicopter involved in the chase.

The motors of the boat roared bravely, then they began to hear dry hits, in gusts. They were shooting at them from the helicopter.

- They're shooting at the engines - said Lázaro.

- They already hit both of them, I have no pressure. Sorry, brother, there is nothing else to do. Yoel said as he raised his hands, a clear gesture of surrender for the bullets to stop.

The other crew members did the same, they waited for the authorities with their hands up. Six uniformed men, visibly upset, boarded the boat, put everyone in handcuffs and sat them next to the engines.

Sad and very tired Yoel told his companions:

- Don't worry, gentlemen, now we are going to have 3 hot and good quality meals, a good bed and general medical assistance, which many in this world would like to have.

- But we are not going to have the most important thing, we are not going to have freedom - Manolo told him.

- You can't have everything - Yoel replied and the whole group laughed.

- Yes brother that is the truth, to God what is God's, and to Caesar what is Caesar's - Manolo told them.

This was the first time any of the four had fallen into the hands of the law. Luckily, the cargo they were carrying came with a prize: the owners of the merchandise had agreed with them that they would pay the bond and the cost of the lawyer in exchange for a reduction in the price of transportation. Instead of charging him $100 per pound shipped, Lazaro and Yoel charged him only $80. The whole group was going to be released on bail until the trial begins, so they were relatively calm when, handcuffed, they were put on the Coast Guard patrol bound for jail.

The four were taken to the Customs Service, where they were asked questions, especially Juan Carlos. They put special pressure on him, because as he was younger they thought he would loosen up, but they were wrong.

Juan Carlos behaved very elegantly, the others did not even open their mouths to yawn, they limited themselves to giving their general information: name, date of birth and address. They all knew that they would soon have a lawyer on their side and that reassured them. Although they also knew very well how the investigators operated, this time there were no problems.

A little later they were handed over to the US Marshals, and in the morning they appeared before a US federal magistrate and were charged with the crimes of possession and conspiracy to distribute controlled substances. Bail was set at $100,000 each, and from there they were taken to the Miami federal prison at SW 137th Avenue and 160th Street.

Already sitting quietly in his cell, Yoel said to Lázaro:

- They are going to put pressure on Juan Carlos to say who owns the merchandise.

- Don't worry that Juan Carlos isn't going to say anything to him, he has character and besides this is yerba and they give you months for yerba, and for a few months no one slacks off. If they were 30 years, another rooster would crow.

Already very tired, they did something that they had not been able to achieve in 3 days: they went to sleep, and in less than 5 minutes, sleep and fatigue transported them to the kingdom of Morpheus, non-stop.

The next day they received a visit from the lawyer A. Portela, who told them:

- We can file a motion to lower his bail, but the old man does not want to wait, he has told us that this is not what was agreed upon. He wants you guys out tomorrow, today the bail bondsman should come to get you out, around 4 in the afternoon. Please be patient. -

When the lawyer left the cell, Yoel said to Lázaro:

- We have done very well in negotiating 80 percent, these lawyers seem good and the bail bondsmen have the rest.

That night, at the bail bond office, old Pedro, who had flown in Alberto's plane to bring him a little present, was waiting for them.

- Well, guys, I've brought you a gift of 10 thousand dollars so you can spend Christmas, but I also want to ask you - Lázaro interrupted him and said:

- You don't have to ask Pedro anything, what's left over there we have to bring here, we're going to wait for December to pass and in January we'll be back at it, maybe with more luck.

Lázaro arrived at his house, hugged his wife and his children, and once again remembered why he did what he did.

- How did things turn out? - she asked him.

"They went well," she said briefly.

- But they were imprisoned! she told him, surprised by her husband's response.

- Don't you see me here, love? I'm alive and kicking - Lázaro replied.

He rested for a few hours and the next day, very early, he left in his other boat to look for 15,000 pounds of marijuana that had been stuck in the Bahamas.

In his new dance with the waves and fate, he recalled a passage from "The Old Man and the Sea," his favorite work by Ernest Hemingway:

"A man is not made for defeat; a man can be destroyed but not defeated."

EPISODE 2

FAST MONEY, BUT NOT EASY

That morning, Yoel and Lázaro sat on the dock at the Crandon Park marina waiting for the arrival of the special envoy and trusted man of the Murillo brothers, the owners of the job they had to do that day.

On the other side of the water stood majestically the city of Miami, vibrant, full of life and warmth. But that landscape for these two men was invisible. They had been on those shores for so long that they lost the capacity for amazement that many people feel when they look at that architectural spectacle of cement and Hispanic heritage. It is the same thing that happens to an office worker when he spends 8 hours every day in front of a window with a view of the sea, there comes a time when the landscape no longer registers an emotion in his mind.

The job that day for these two "clerks" was to find a sailboat in the North Channel lighthouse, a place where the bank of the Bahama Islands meets the tongue of the Atlantic Ocean. The depths of the tongue allow large cruise ships to visit the island of New Providence, where the city of Nassau, the capital of the Bahamas Islands, is located. Yoel and Lázaro, after finding the sailboat, had to bring their cargo to Florida.

They had already been waiting for more than half an hour, when they saw someone running towards the entrance to the pier, waving their arms. When the distance was shortened they realized that the one running to meet them was someone well known. But he was not who they expected.

Running, almost desperate, as if he were being chased by a rabid dog, came Silvio Lugo, a fellow political prisoner in Cuba and a friend of both. He had come to the United States through Mariel, just like Lázaro.

- Look who's coming by the dock - said Yoel and added: - What is this character doing here at this hour and running like crazy?

"I can't imagine it," Lázaro replied to his companion, "but he doesn't have a good face, something strange is happening."

They didn't have to wait long to find out why they were in such a hurry, because at one point Silvio came up to them, greeted them and said:

- Good thing I arrived on time, before you had set sail. - Said the newcomer trying to catch his breath. - I went by Yoel's house and they told me that you had left for this marina because you had plans to go fishing today, that the bonito is running and I came running and praying that they had not gone to sea.

- Is it true that the beautiful one is running? Lázaro asked.

- Of course partner, you don't watch the television news, all the channels have a space dedicated to fishing, remember that Miami is a city of the sea - Yoel said with a half smile. Then he turned to Silvio and asked him:

- And what is your run-run and yelling, brother?

- Boy, I have a tremendous problem, - Silvio replied as the colors returned to his face, already a little recovered from the rush - a tremendous problem.

"That's nothing new, Silvio, we all have problems," Lázaro replied sarcastically.

-Yes, but mine is so big that it can cost me my head.

- If it can cost you your head, then your problem is very big - answered Yoel, now worried.

- But tell us, to see what we can help you with, because that's why I'm sure you've come to see us, haven't you? - Lázaro added, already speaking very seriously.

- Yes, they are right - Silvio replied - and the only ones who can help me are you.

- Don't heat up the patch anymore and just let it go - Yoel told him impatiently.

- Guys I tell you that I have a cat in the air a DC3, commercial ID number 3, with 1000 school notebooks. And the boatmen that I had hired, after taking the money for the expenses, now say that their equipment is broken, and they can't do the job for me. I am embarked.

A lot of sweat ran down Silvio's face, but he didn't know if it was because of the previous race plus the Miami heat or because of the panic that made him know that if he couldn't pick up that load he was going to get into tremendous trouble.

"A thousand school notebooks" was, in the jargon of smugglers, a thousand pounds of marijuana, just under 500 kilos.

- And why didn't you come to see us first? - Yoel asked him, and Lázaro almost didn't let him finish, he gave him the answer that everyone knew:

- We are very expensive, brother, I am sure that they are Mickey Mouse, that the contract was much cheaper.

- I'm not going to lie to you, you're right, that's why the proverb doesn't fail and they say that cheap is expensive, look what I'm involved in now - Silvio said with his eyes wide open, as if begging for a positive answer.

- Your problem is really big, because we have a commitment for today, and you found us here by chance. Lázaro explained. - We are here waiting for the special envoy of our client, who seems to be in the arms of morpheus, and it has not arrived yet, because at this time we should already be fishing bonito.

- But if it's not indiscretion, how many are you going for this time? Silvio asked him.

Yoel replied: - Let's go for 2,000 notebooks from your same school.

- This horse can handle 6,000 notebooks - Silvio said and added: - Remember that I am putting my life in your hands, and you know that I have a family, a wife, and small children.

"Don't dramatize, brother, I'm going to cry," Yoel said trying to soften the emotions of the moment, and turning to Lázaro, he asked him: "What do you think about this case, do you think we can break the rich today?" Because really Silvio is very right, and the horse can carry it, the horse can fit more than 6,000 notebooks?

When Lázaro said the horse, he was referring to a 37-foot Mira, with powerful 370-horsepower Mercury engines, which was tied to the dock, which was his work tool.

- But there is no problem of cargo space, it is a problem of time and place - Lázaro clarified. - And also that Manolo and Rosendo wait for us again to load 2000 notebooks, and we can't show up with 5000.

- Yes, but we can leave part of the work stuck in the bush and, well, what we put in the fishmonger's truck.

Silvio listened to this talk between the two friends without picking up a word, or a gesture, with his heart in his mouth. He knew what it could cost him if they didn't agree.

- It's okay - Lázaro finally said and, addressing Silvio, extended his hand and added: - Get off with the 4 lucas that the book says for expenses.

The newcomer smiled for the first time that morning, relieved. Then he turned serious again, they were about to talk about money, and they don't joke about that.

- The boatmen left me bare. I only have $3,000 left. I don't think you guys will let me die for a grand. Silvio replied thinking about what the Colombian drug traffickers would do to him if he did not complete the operation as agreed.

Drug trafficking, even marijuana, has always been associated with acts of extreme cruelty, such as messages to those who are alive so that they never dare to betray the ringleaders. Death used to be the best option in those cases.

- Silvio is fine - Lázaro replied - but we still haven't talked about the most important thing. How much are you going to pay us? -

- How much will they charge me? Silvio asked.

- 25% of the merchandise on the shore - answered Yoel.

- Guys, they're hitting me against the wall. If I give them that, I gain nothing! Silvio said.

- It could be, but we are charging you a fine for having cheated on those men - Yoel said a little jokingly, but also very seriously.

- Look Silvio, for being our colleague from the provincial prison of Pinar del Río we are going to throw you in the towel, and we are going to charge you only 20%. Lázaro told him. - And let there be no more talk of money. But now you give me the pasta and sit here next to us to wait for the Indian, who must be there when he arrives.

Silvio took out 3,000 dollars in a pile of 5 and 10 bills, which Lázaro, not counting, threw into a briefcase, and said:

- This money is black money, five and dollar bills, neighborhood sale money, don't tell me you're selling little bags.

- No compadre, this was given to me by the owners of the merchandise - Silvio replied. Yoel pointing to the entrance of the pier said:

- Look, gentlemen, the man from the Murillo brothers is coming in from the pier.

Indeed, entering the pier, there was the Colombian, a young man of about 30 years of age, tall and thin, of decent appearance, with a briefcase in his hand.

Lázaro commented:

- Look at the size of the briefcase that Jairo brings. He really believes that we are going on vacation to the Bahamas.

- They're like that and you're not going to change them, and don't waste time telling them, because we're never going to be able to change it - Yoel replied.

The Colombian arrived with them and, almost without saying a word, the entire group boarded the boat.

The ropes were released, the fenders were hauled in, and the launch detached itself from the dock. Silvio and Jairo occupied the stern seat, next to the engines, Yoel took the helm, and Lázaro stood next to him, supervising everything.

They passed under the bridge that connects the Miami Seaquarium to the Crandon Park marina, and into the open water. They set a course 90° East on the compass, or compass, toward the island of Bimini, the first stop on their journey, where they planned to have lunch. They would go to the little restaurant of the black mom, the brunette, that Pancho had introduced them to a few years earlier, with whom they had made a very good friendship.

The island of South Bimini and North Bimini forms a small archipelago, and is located 50 sea miles from Miami, to the east of the Florida Peninsula, and with a population that does not exceed ten thousand people, mostly made up of blacks, descendants of slaves that the English brought from Africa in those days.

Today the small islands have grown a lot. In those days there were about five or six hotels, 4 or 5 marinas, a couple of restaurants, no more than six small discotheques-bars, 5 or 6 small shops, a power plant, a customs office, and a small police station, with a few agents.

The easiest thing to find on the island, apart from tourists and fishermen, almost all gringos, were the smugglers, mostly Cubans and Colombians; and its counterpart, the American law enforcement officers.

Sometimes you didn't know who was who. Covertly they spied on everything. Drug smuggling was already in the sights of the United States government and they knew the routes very well. It was logical that they had their spies everywhere, always trying to discover who moved more merchandise, how, when and where.

That is why it was very important to know how to pretend to be a tourist or a fisherman. At that time, the Bahamas were a paradise for anyone from Miami who liked fishing, had money and a boat to get there, whether it was the Cuban or gringo middle class, those who practiced the divine charm of the bourgeoisie.

Another phenomenon that happened in those days was that the constant harassment by the Yankee authorities forced the traffickers to leave the Islands and move to Mexico, where they benefited from easy access to the United States. Far from eradicating evil, they ended up multiplying it, as they say, 'a troubled river, profit for fishermen'. Many traffickers operating from the Bahamas moved to Mexico where their profits multiplied due to easy access across the border. The fever attracted many others in search of good fortune which gave rise to another bigger problem for the gringos, now known as "the Mexican drug cartels".

The Bahamas had another problem in the 1980s: the corruption of the authorities of the Islands, who always wanted to get a slice of the cake. That is natural if there is poverty, on the one hand, and a lot of money on the other. In other words, it was an extremely hot place, and not just because it was in the Caribbean. You had to watch out for your own shadow.

The day was sunny and the sea was calm, ideal for crossing the channel enjoying the sea breeze. Only a couple of merchant ships crossed in the entire navigation.

Already around midday, Lázaro, Yoel, Silvio and Jairo, the Colombian, spotted the pine trees on the island and headed for the entrance channel. This body of water runs parallel to South Bimini, practically dividing the island in two. They docked at the Big Game Marina Hotel, proceeded to Customs and Immigration, and after filling out all the proper paperwork and tipping the Bahamian government official a hundred dollars so he wouldn't ask too many questions, they received the entry permit for the boat and immigration for the four of them. They were also given a sport fishing license.

With everything in order, they headed to their friend's cubbyhole or small restaurant.

They arrived at the place and after greeting the brunette, they sat down at some rustic tables in the place and Yoel asked her in Spanish:

- Mom, what do we have today for lunch?

"Chicken, meat, rice, potato salad," the brunette responded in her broken Spanish learned through machetes during her daily dealings with the Cuban boatmen and the Colombian companions, her most frequent clientele.

Colombian Jairo asked Yoel in a low voice: - Is this the best place to have a quality lunch?

- It's not the best, but it's the safest for those of us who don't come here as tourists or underwater fishermen. Yes, of course there are more elegant and much more expensive places than this, but much more dangerous. They are full of undercover agents of the three letters, who are here to monitor our steps, and especially if we are Latinos, Cubans and Colombians, because they see us as illegal or worse.

- And what do you consider as something worse than us? Jairo asked jokingly.

- A politician for example - replied Yoel smiling - but don't play dumb, you know very well what I mean, and the funniest thing is that you're not far from being right.

-Besides, -Mom interrupted with the air of having overheard inadvertently and showing that she had learned a lot of Spanish- I cook very tasty, and I think I charge half of what they would have to pay elsewhere.

- You see, Jairo - Silvio replied to the Colombian - your rudeness has hurt our friend's feelings, and besides, Mom is absolutely right about that, because she lets them taste her food so that you realize what we are telling you. we say.-

- I'm not saying that mom doesn't cook well, but I'm tired of eating meat and chicken, which is what I always eat in Miami. Today I want to eat something else.

- What do you want to eat, Jairo? Yoel asked him, and the Colombian did not wait, neither slow nor lazy, he said: - I want to eat a seafood jelly, with lobsters and fish.

Lázaro looked at Mama with a certain tenderness and a little remorse for the low prices and said:

- Mom prepares a seafood dish with as many irons as possible.

"Of course it's possible, it's just that she's going to take a little longer," the black woman replied.

- And how much longer? -asked Silvio worried about his DC3, flying with the 3000 notebooks inside it.

"About an hour or so," black Mama told him.

"Okay," Yoel told him, "we have time." - and looking back at Silvio I ask him: - Is your work between the two lights?

For the smugglers between the two lights means that it was late afternoon, twilight time. Each guild has a way of saying their things.

- Yes, mine is between the two lights, but remember that we still have to get to the point. Silvio replied.

- Give me the paper with the numbers - asked Lázaro.

Silvio handed him a dollar bill with some numbers written in pen, which Lázaro read and then said: - It's not that we have too much time, but if we can buy and then get to the place, before your bird.

The black Mama went to give the order to make the seafood and when Lázaro returned, he called her and asked:

- Bold you haven't told us, how is the island these days?

- It's very hot. We have people who were born here, because it seems that they are waiting for something big that you know is becoming fashionable. I think someone has given them a good whistle - Mom replied.

- And what is becoming fashionable? - Silvio asked him, not missing a word of the conversation.

- You know very well - the black woman told him - Snow White with the seven dwarfs. And I ask you to be very careful, and on your way back, pass as far away as possible from the islands. Get as far away as you can from the blacks in Nassau, they are very dangerous. Don't let them scare you.

- Thank you, mom - Lázaro told her and went to help prepare the seafood jelly that Colombian Jairo had wanted to eat.

- Do you have a lot of trust with her? Jairus asked him.

- If a good friend introduced us to her a long time ago, and he told us that she has a son who is imprisoned in the United States. And she is convinced that the boy didn't do anything, that they fabricated a case for him to take time away from a boss in your country, Yoel replied.
- And how can the gringos do that? Jairus asked.

- It's very easy - Lázaro responded quickly - someone set a trap for the boy, like 1 kg of parrot and alerted the United States authorities. And for that collaboration they give the infamous a reduced sentence.

"But that's not fair, that's immoral," answered Jairo with a little fear on his face.
.

- And who told you that humanity is good, that men are just, and women are grateful - answered Yoel.

- And whose thought is it? Jairus asked.

Lázaro told him: - Yoel doesn't even respect the photo, because that thought more or less belongs to José Martí, but the true thought is: You have to think that humanity is good, that men are just, and that homeland is grateful

Yoel took the floor: - A long time ago a good friend, who unfortunately is no longer with us, introduced us to her. And he himself told us that his mother has a son in prison, in the United States federal prison, because they caught him at the Miami airport, with 1 kg of it, and gave him a 5-year sentence. That is why the gringos are not saints of his devotion. She is a mother at last and her children are born forgiven. She says that they set a trap for her black boy. I think that innocent, as innocent, he is not, because he should have known what he was doing to him, but coming here to the island and proposing a business to someone and knowing that someone is a poor man, and then waiting for him in Miami, putting him prisoner, and give him five years in prison, I don't know what to tell you. I think it is an injustice and for her it is more injustice, because she is her mother. See if she sees it as an injustice that there aren't any blondes here having lunch. This cubbyhole is exclusive for people of the guild. -

The four men continued talking about various topics until Mama's helper came with the special fish and seafood dish, which had lobsters, conch, shrimp, squid, octopus; In short, all the delicacies of the sea accompanied by a rich potato salad, with lots of black pepper, in the purest Bahamian style.

The whole group ate quickly. In the end Yoel left a $100 bill on the table. Jairo surprised asked him:

- And that seafood dish is worth so much money?

- No friend - Lázaro said and burst out laughing. - Where did the Murillo family get this naive creature? The seafood platter is worth 50 dollars, the other 50 dollars is for information, but the tip that is going to be left is still missing. you put the bills on the table so that the black woman knows you and trusts you, because don't forget that money wins women's trust. And Mom is a woman, she is no exception to the rule.

Jairo, against his wishes, took a $20 bill out of his pocket and left it on the table, littered with dirty dishes, fish bones, and empty lobster heads.

Then they said goodbye to mom and left for the dock walking very slowly because of the drowsiness caused by the fullness of everything they had eaten.

Arriving at the boat next to the dock, Lázaro asked the boy in charge of the gas pump:

- Johnny, have you fueled the equipment yet?

The young man replied: - Yes, the total is $180. -

Lázaro gave him two $100 bills and said: - Keep the change and thank you very much. -

- Why so much tip money? Jairo asked again, already bordering on impertinence.

- Gasoline here is 3 dollars a gallon and the rest is a tip - Yoel told him.

"Okay," said the Colombian, and added: "But don't tell me now to leave a $20 tip for Moyetito as well."

- Even if you don't believe it, it's so that I get to know you, in case you come back here one day - Lázaro told him.

- From what I see that in these Islands you have to pay up to laughter - Jairo added with a resigned tone.

-Not only here my friend, it is the same everywhere and everyone here knows what we come to do in these Islands, silence has its price and you have to pay it- Lázaro reflected as he headed towards the boat.

Once everyone was on board, with the help of the little black man, they released the ropes and took the exit channel again, parallel to the island of South Bimini, until reaching the tip of the island. From there they headed for the sunken ship, where, as always, they would find fans of underwater fishing. In 20 minutes they passed the large cement structure anchored in the sand.

Many years before, a ship had sunk, victim of some hurricane that, during the months between August and October, hit the Caribbean Sea; and indeed, next to the sunken ship there were two sailboats and two yachts and several fishermen in the water. And the red and white flags that alert the presence of men fishing in the water are displayed on the boat.

- Why don't we take advantage and go fishing? Yoel said. -To see what Silvio's face looks like,-and he added:- hopefully we'll catch something and make time, it's only 3 in the afternoon.

- I don't know - answered Lázaro - but it seems to me that you want to kill Silvio's nerves. Better we fish at the point, just in case, and wait there. -

Later, Lázaro turned to Silvio and said: - Brother, give me your numbers again. Give me the latitude and longitude of the job. -

Silvio took out of his pocket a dollar bill that had some numbers written on it and handed it to Lázaro.

- 24.42.00 north latitude, 78.18.00 west longitude. It's okay, in 40 minutes we are there, at that point that is written on the ticket. - Lázaro said, showing off his enormous knowledge of the area, as well as the coordinates.

Yoel put 180° on the compass and they took off like lightning at 3500 revolutions per minute. The boat flew through the waves powered by the two 330 horsepower engines, soon reaching 50 miles per hour speed.

The boat sailed over the Bank of the Bahamas to meet the DC 3, which was the aircraft that Silvio had to wait for and that would drop the 3,000 notebooks into the water.

Yoel at the helm and Lázaro next to him, and Jairo and Silvio in the seat next to the engines; Yoel and Lázaro sang an old Spanish song.

> *"With ten cannonry per band,*
> *Wind in their sails,*
> *does not cut the sea, but flies*
> *a brigantine sailing ship…"*

In 40 minutes the boat and its crew were at the meeting point. And Silvio, for the first time that day, was able to breathe easily.

- Guys, drop the anchor, I'm crazy to start fishing - Yoel told them.

Lázaro reacted immediately and said: - We better not drop any anchor and stay at par, in case we have to run away, not lose the anchor, the chain, and a good piece of rope.

This is how the mind of a smuggler works, always alert to the arrival of the law.

- Perfect, at the same time we can fish the line - said the Colombian.

- We can catch some nice snapper and grouper. -And he asked Lázaro: -Did you bring some fishing gear?

- Of course we always bring them. In addition, we bring bait and two buckets of engo. Remember the saying, without engo or bait nothing is caught - replied Lázaro.

In addition, carrying fishing gear was always necessary to avoid suspicion, it was part of the disguise, when the Coast Guard patrols approached.

Yoel and Jairo sat on the cabin of the boat, enjoying Yoel's favorite sport, line fishing. Lázaro and Silvio sat by the engines and suddenly Lázaro asked:

- Partner, tell me the true story in which you were a participant, because there are many versions of it and they are all contradictory.

- What story are you talking about, brother? If we talk about stories, I in particular have participated in many and they all have contradictory versions.

- Don't play dumb or goofy with nonsense because you know what story I'm talking about. I'm talking about that trip to New York in which you accompanied Aracel, the fat man, and Julito, the countryman. And that it cost them both their lives, they were your friends and mine too. You went with them and you know the truth.

Silvio became serious.

- I don't prefer to talk about that. That was a long time ago and it brings back a lot of bad memories. Also, it is very dangerous to talk about it.

He paused and looked at the horizon, as if he were looking for an answer in the vastness of the sea. He continued.

- But now I am indebted to you for this favor that you are doing me, and I am going to make an exception and I am going to please you; and you will receive the real version of the only survivor of the problem, the version of one of its protagonists. -

CHAPTER 3

THE DEATH OF ARACEL, EL GORDO AND JULITO, EL PAISANO

Silvio settled on the edge of the boat and felt that a very ancient electricity ran through his body. The faces of his two friends came to mind. He remembered them with sorrow, but also feeling that the fate they suffered was not his fault. He knew perfectly well that, by a miracle, the 3 did not die. Someone had to tell the story, it was his turn.

- A few years ago, the three of us, Aracel the fat man, Julito the countryman, and I were newcomers to the United States and alone. You didn't have that situation because you came to this country with your wife and children, but it sucks to be alone in a country where you don't even speak the language. A cold country and perhaps a little materialistic.

- A little, I would say a lot - Lázaro replied.

- Don't interrupt me and let me continue. The three of us, Julito, Aracel and I had rented a small apartment in Little Havana. I tell you between the three of us to be able to pay the rent, to be able to have a roof over our heads and a kitchen to prepare something to eat. And there we try to survive as we could. We did whatever work it was, construction, mechanics, bodywork, whatever came, but in reality we were eating Nicolás by one leg, we were eating tremendous cable, and sometimes we didn't even have cable to eat. In order not to die of boredom, sadness and loneliness, we began to visit a bar, which I believe is still there on Northwest 7th Street at the corner of 24th Avenue. The bar is Quisqueya, owned by a Dominican named Pedro and there we met a Colombian who said his name was Henry.

- To combat sadness and loneliness they ended up in a bar - Lázaro reproached him and added -: Why didn't they go to a church?

- Do not criticize me my brother and better understand me that you are not a saint either, because if you were a saint now we would not be here and we would be in a church. Let me continue, if you already lost me in the story, let me do it - Silvio said with a nervous tone, as if the past was playing a bad joke on him.

- It's true, but we human beings are prone to see the speck in someone else's eye and not the beam in our own. It is true that bandits don't go to church until life passes them by and then they understand and repent. Hopefully it's not too late for us -Lazaro told him. And he added: "Okay Silvio, continue your story."

- As I have told you in that vice and prostitution called the Quisqueya, all that was gathered was shrapnel, and here we met, as I have already told you, a certain Henry. And between drinks and parakeet passes we establish a certain friendship or complicity, because in those places it is rare to find a friend, but it is to be expected to find an accomplice.

Silvio stopped and told Lázaro -: Wait a minute and let me put the 2-meter radius on, in case the device calls us, be alert, because it's about time and he must be arriving in the area, well if you haven't had any news.

Silvio stood up and went to the cabin of the boat. He went into it and brought a small briefcase from which he took out a 2 meter handheld radio with crystals to prevent interference. Already by that time the 2-meter radios had replaced the blue ones to communicate with the planes from the boats or from the ground. He also took a battery-powered rotating lantern with a red light from the briefcase and placed it on the boat's console. He returned and sat down again next to Lázaro and said to him:

- I hope we have luck today, and the device, and well?

Like a bolt of lightning, Lázaro replied: - I hope you haven't made us come here today, for pleasure. -

- What do you want? You well know what this business is like, with dirt runways lit up with streaks of oil and drunken gringo pilots. Anything can happen, you know that commercial planes with well-lit asphalt runways and good fuel crash, what do you expect with our teams? You've been to Colombia and you've seen with your own eyes what it's like there - Silvio replied.

"Yes, I've really had to live that experience," Lázaro replied.

- The planes that are rattled, are regularly parked on the island of Aruba or Curacao. From there they fly to Colombia and have to land in the middle of the night on dirt runways, lit with wisps of tow and oil; and, in addition, to pick up the load, which you know what it is, often gasoline contaminated with water. In that job of the pilots, more than 50% cannot get paid because the job falls out or is stolen. And they call that easy money, it might be quick money, but easy, it's not - Silvio told him.

- There's nothing easy about it - confirmed Lázaro and added: - I've already lost several fellow pilots in this business, Facenda and Ibarras, two Cuban pilots, and a Lebanese. Also, a very good friend, Mario the Bearded died because, when he was taking off, his load shifted and the plane crashed. A good man with a wife and three children, but let's return to the subject of our conversation.

- Well, I'll continue telling you, this individual named Henry told us that someone owed him two million dollars from a business in New York City, the Big Apple. And that he was being silly and grumpy to pay the money. Henry told us that he was looking for someone brave enough to go to New York to collect. He was offering a 300,000-peso reward, and you know, saying that to us, three crazy people who were starving, is like showing a rabbit to a lion. Put yourself in our place, alone, without family and eating a cable, and that person gives us the opportunity to earn 300,000 pesos in a few days, that cannot be missed.

- Julito told Henry that he could count on us, but that he had to give us the means to carry out the operation: a car to travel north, money for expenses, food, gasoline and a hotel. Silvio said and continued.

- Henry told us to make a plan and come back the next day to pursue the matter. That night we couldn't sleep, partly because of hunger and partly because of emotion. I already saw myself with a new Cadillac, a gold Saint Lázaro medallion and a diamond around my neck, and a Rolex watch on my wrist. In our minds, the three of us spent the reward money and I even made a plan to bring my mother and my brothers from Cuba, because I assure you that the family is greatly needed.

They heard a noise in the night and Silvio stopped counting, but nothing, it was a false alarm. They were the engines of a commercial plane at high altitude, Silvio continued.

- The next day we all went to the Quisqueya bar to interview Henry, who was always accompanied by a group of hitmen, all armed to the teeth. Of course, I suspected. He thought: how strange that within that element there was no one who was willing to do the work of collecting the money, but the need or the ambition did not allow us to reflect well and we decided to go ahead with the plan. I thought that it could be that the Colombian Henry would trust us more than them, because I really believe that none of those cheap criminals would have returned after collecting the bill, from a briefcase with two million pesos inside, and they would deliver it to him to Henry, of tame dove.

- Julito el paisa told the Colombian that the plan was very simple, that he give us the means, the car, the money and the iron, that we would take care of doing the rest: Go to New York City, find the man , grab him by the neck and force him

to pay the money. How naive of us, Henry told us with a sarcastic smile, "you think it's so easy, but I'm going to trust you. I'm going to give them a car, a brand new Monte Carlo Chevrolet, I'm going to give them three 45 caliber pistols and five thousand dollars for gas, hotel and food expenses. With that money they should have left over if they don't buy parrots or drink drinks, which I can't forbid, but I can recommend that they don't do it during work."

At this point in the story and knowing the kind of mobsters in that business, Lázaro was already beginning to imagine the end.

Silvio continued with his story as if he were living it in his head.

- Mr. Henry, we don't have as much left as you say, - I told him - because if we don't find the man, the first day we are going to have to spend several days looking for him and the Big Apple is not called that for pleasure. According to my calculations, that city has more than 23 million inhabitants and we are not going to take such a long trip to return empty-handed. I find it, even if I have to rent a hotel and stay there for a whole month, I didn't return to Miami without that money.

- Just like my partner Silvio said - answered Julito and added -: And if things get complicated and we can't stay in a hotel, we stay in the central park to sleep. Those who have been there, in that place, have told me that it is very cold, but we will have to be cold.

- "That's how I like it guys, - said the Colombian Henry - I want you to have that same fighting spirit, but don't worry: if that happens, I'll send you more money through Western Union. I really like your enthusiasm. I believe that you are going to be successful in this company, but since now everything is already discussed, have a beer that I invite you, and today give each other a few hits, a few little walks of yeyo, because later you will have to refrain. I repeat, along the way you must not take or drink, or drugs of any kind, because if by chance of life they stop you for any reason, they find drugs and weapons, I am not going to answer for that, let it be well Clear." Although what Mr. Henry asked from us was very difficult to do, we promised him, because compromising is easy. We agreed on everything and left the next day after Henry had given them the car, the guns, and the money for expenses.

- And what cars did he give them?- Lázaro asked.

-He gave us a white Montecarlo of the year, weapons and money for expenses. That same afternoon we got wasted and we all screwed up at the invitation of the Colombian. We arrived at the apartment at 1:00 in the morning. Julito and I fell flat on the bed from exhaustion and intoxication. But Aracel left with one of the Central American girls from the bar, a Titi, as he called her. With the commitment to be ready the next day, I don't think the fat man could sleep that night, with the confrontation he had.

- And Aracel complied? Did he arrive on time? - Lázaro asked.

- Wait and I'll tell you - Silvio continued -: The next day we got up early and in a Cuban coffee maker that we had in the kitchen of the apartment, we strained Cuban coffee while we waited for our friend and associate Aracel, the fat one, who He arrived in time to drink the coffee I had made and it was still hot. After having coffee, we went out very excited to collect the weapons, the money and the car to leave immediately for New York. As an old proverb says: "He who climbs on the back of a tiger only has one problem, getting off it."

Henry had made an appointment for us at noon, at the La Perla Del Mar restaurant on 7th Street and 44th Avenue. We arrived at the place, parked our transportation and sat down in the restaurant to wait for the man who arrived accompanied by two other Colombians, two Barranquilleros like him, and introduced us to those who accompanied him.

-This gentleman is Salim and his friend Pacho. Salim and Pacho are my partners in the business and what you are going to charge is more theirs than mine, that's why I took the audacity to bring them to meet you. I think you have no problem or objection to it. In particular, the faces of those two characters didn't bother me at all, but at the height of the game with those two pints in front of me, which I could do and I replied: - We don't have any problem getting to know them, for the Otherwise, it is an honor. We entered the restaurant and sat down for lunch. Henry told us: - I have the car outside - and the rest is inside. The three of us sat together.

We all ordered oysters, grouper soup, and baked fish filet. We ordered more or less the same, except for Julito who ordered fried squid. The Colombian Pacho told us: - Eat well boys, a long trip awaits you. Take advantage of Henry's invitation and give way to his taste. -

-Julito, taking him at his word, ordered two portions of fried shrimp and two portions of fried conch and 6 very cold beers. Henry reminded us: - Eat all you want, but just one beer. Remember that you have to drive and if you drive, don't drink and if you drink, don't drive, as the propaganda says. -

-It was markedly evident that he was very interested in us reaching New York. After lunch they went out to the parking lot of La Perla Del Mar restaurant and as Henry had promised, he handed her the key to a white 1981 Chevrolet Monte Carlo with only 10,000 miles on it. He gave her the money and the three 45-caliber pistols with the serial numbers erased, and the three Colombians said goodbye. We asked Henry to be aware of seeing the telephone of the bar, owned by Pedro the Dominican. The bar belonged to Pedro, but Henry managed it. -

- "Henry, - I told him, already mounted in the brand new white Montecarlo - keep an eye on the phone in the bar office in case any problem arises and we have to consult with you. - Don't worry, guys - Pacho answered us - Henry will be aware of the phone. -

-Aracel, the fat one, who was the best driver among us, because in Cuba he worked driving a cargo truck on the highway, he took the wheel of the vehicle that had been delivered to us with a full tank of gasoline. We got on the Dolphin Expressway to meet I-95 North, which was to take us to our final destination, the capital of the world, the city of great skyscrapers, the immense and cosmopolitan city of New York. The one that since that time would be the city of traps. -

- Pushed by our intrepidity and youth we got on that cannonball, we traveled flying down the Expressway, feeling like the owners of the world, as if the money was already in our pockets. About 8:00 at night we passed Jacksonville in North Florida. Julito suggested that we go into a Denny's restaurant next to the road and Aracel the fat man recommended: - Why don't we take a little detour to eat the best fried rice in the whole country? -

- I asked him: - Where do you eat that fried rice? - In the city of Savannah in Georgia.

- I don't believe you, - I replied - as far as I know the best fried rice in the country is eaten in the city of San Francisco, California.

- "Faint in that size" (cuban saying for no way) - Julito told us and added: - The best made fried rice is eaten in New York City's Chinatown. When we get to the Big Apple I'm going to show it to you.

- Don't talk any more nonsense, gentlemen, we are going to go to San Francisco and we still have time to get to New York. Let's go into a Denny's I'm starving, we'll see later. -

- We got off I-95 and went into a Denny's, had dinner and got back on the road. We passed Georgia, South Carolina and then North. In Washington we fill up with gas and decide to go to one of the many hotels along the highway to sleep. Our best driver, the fat one, was very tired from

the drive and from the bad night the day before. Well if
what had happened to him, he could be called a bad night.
The next morning, we had breakfast at a waffle house and
then headed back on the road. We passed over the
Potomac River and saw the White House, the Lincoln
Memorial, and the United States Capitol in the distance.
Hours later we were racing down the New Jersey Turnpike,
passing through the Lincoln Tunnel and entering our
destination in the Big Apple, New York City. We are about
to climb on the back of the tiger, which could only be
fought with great cunning and with great luck. -

- We finally arrived at the famous World Trade Center. We
entered a tower, oriented with the address and name that
Henry had marked us on the 81st floor of the building. We
took the elevator, like a supersonic plane, and he took us
to where we wanted. In a few minutes we were in front of
an elegant office with a sign that said Marder Inversiones.
We walked in and talked to a receptionist. I assumed that
she was bilingual and she asked us in Spanish with a
Puerto Rican accent: -What do you gentlemen want? -
I took command of the operation so as not to let the
deceased speak because I understood that their loud voice
and style of saying things would be a bit convenient, at that
time and in that place.

- Good afternoon, miss, we want to talk to Mr. Alfonso
Ospina, please - I told her.

- Do you have an appointment or is Mr. Ospina waiting for
you? - The receptionist asked me, a girl with the face of a
doll and the body of a Barbie. Now I was convinced that
she was Puerto Rican, as I had always said, there is no
ugly Puerto Rican.

- No, we don't have an appointment, but please tell Mr. Ospina that there are some friends of Mr. Henry Monsalvo here who want to talk to him.

- The girl called another secretary who told us: - Please, gentlemen, sit down and wait. If the gentlemen wish, I can offer you coffee or a soft drink. Julito did not miss the opportunity to wreak some havoc and told the girl: - Yes, of course doll, we want coffee and if you can also bring some biscuits. -

- Behind the receptionist there was a large painting with an inscription, in a language I did not know, but I was interested to know what that strange inscription said. I thought it would be in Arabic or some Asian, Persian or Hindustani language; but I was left with the doubt. A few minutes later, another young woman came in with the same bearing as the Puerto Rican and with the same accent, and she served us coffee, water, and some biscuits. And Aracel whispered in my ear:
- This guy should hire the employees by catalog, do you buy them made or have them made? - They both smiled mischievously.

- I replied: - What is needed is not a catalog, what is needed is the ticket. If one day you get a ticket, you're also going to have pretty secretaries - the phone rang and the Puerto Rican receptionist answered it and said: - Gentlemen, Mr. Ospina is waiting for you, please follow me. -

- Without knowing it, we were already on top of the Bengal tiger, one of the most dangerous predators on the planet.

We entered a corridor with offices to the right and to the left, on the wall of the corridor there was another painting just like the one that hung behind the wall. The receptionist already intrigued me what that strange inscription said, because surely those paintings must contain some subliminal message. We followed the secretariat knowing that if Alfonso Ospina did not tell me what the posters said, I would ask him. We arrived at a large office with glass windows from where I could see the Hudson River and part of the city. The office was furnished, elegantly and soberly, one would say with the class that money brings. Behind a mahogany desk an insignificant-looking man for he was short in stature not to weigh my 150 pounds, red-haired, white-skinned, about 30 years old, neatly dressed in a simple white shirt and blue tie, and He asked us: - Well, gentlemen, what can I do for you? What is the reason for your visit? What business can I advise you on? What business are you interested in investing in? Buying real estate or shares of the stock market?

Her tone was friendly and relaxed. She could tell that she didn't dislike us or our visit she was enjoying. Contrary to a bad feeling, she enjoyed our presence. I would say it was more folkloric and sympathy for us.

I took the initiative and the word again and told him:

- We come from Mr. Henry Monsalvo, whom you must know. - The boy answered us in perfect Spanish, which I would say with a small accent of Cuban origin.

- Of course I know Mr. Henry Monsalvo. He is a client and partner of mine, as well as my personal friend. What is the message that you bring me from him? -

I took the floor again and told him directly and bluntly: - Mr. Ospina, your client, your partner and your personal friend, Mr. Henry commissioned us to bring you an amount of money to Miami, which, according to him, you owe him. and that according to him has been delayed in paying him.

- Ospina interrupted me and said: - And what is the amount of money that according to Henry I owe him, and I have been late in paying him? His tone of voice was still soft and low, and he looked very calm and relaxed like the one in total control of the situation. -According to Mr. Henry, he told me that it is 2 million dollars.

-Over time and after meeting Alfonso I was convinced that he was a great actor. Alfonso looked at me with a face of not believing what I was saying: - And why hasn't Mr. Henry come to collect that money, himself? -Julito took the floor and said: -Mr. Henry is very busy and we have come to his place.

- I understand, - Alfonso told us- you are Henry's bounty collectors, his collectors, but I am going to be honest with you, because I like you, I like you because really you are going very hungry in Miami and you are very crazy or very brave, because sometimes hunger drives people crazy. -

Silvio's face changed completely, you could already see the tension in his mouth, the muscles of his face, already more rigid, foreshadowed a dramatic ending. Or he was reliving some of the mistakes that the 3 of them had made in those days.

- Alfonso had disrespected us. He had blatantly called us starving, and in those words had shown no respect for Henry or us. He was trying to buy us, he was trying to humiliate us and he was trying to scare us. Alfonso continued: - You came here because I let you come. And they're going to get out of here alive, if I let them out. - Do you know well what you are telling us? - he said to Aracel. And Alfonso replied: - Yes, of course I know, and I also know that you come armed with pistols and you are also brave and have bad intentions, but I also know that you are very intelligent. -

- There was total silence in that office and Alfonso resumed the word: - If you really came armed, I would not have let you get here. You may think that I would put my life in danger. - What Alfonso said left me completely frozen. And he continued: -The 45 pistol that you bring, they have blank bullets. Among Henry's henchmen there are people who answer to me. They put what I advise. So, think carefully about what you are going to do, because, dear countrymen, now you are in trouble and from here you can go straight to the river, melted into a block of cement. I believe that the most advisable thing we can do is to behave like civilized people and negotiate. -

- The word negotiate took my blood to the body and I saw a hope of being able to preserve life if I acted intelligently and the devil would let us escape. I know that this seems more like a story taken from a movie script than a true story and one of its protagonists is telling it to you. As the poem says, "but I'm on my way and no one will separate me, I'm no one's flatter, I have to tell the truth, there is no imitation here, this is pure reality. I asked Alfonso: - How do you say to negotiate if you have four aces in your hand? "Yes, I'm going to negotiate your ransom," he replied with a smile that made my hair stand on end and what you know in my mouth.

Julito was very reckless, he took the floor and told Alfonsito: - Now it turns out that we are the ones who should. I don't think Henry will give our life a single penny. - Ospina continued: - Well now you are the ones in a bad situation, because who can deny me that I paid you the money and you went with him, but to do that I would have to eliminate you. Luckily I am a man of peace and I hate violence that ends badly in the end. I have nothing to gain by melting it down into a concrete block and throwing it in the bottom of the Hudson River and then someone else comes along and does the same thing to me. -

- Alfonso spoke to us, as incredible as it seems to you, more like a preacher than like a mobster. I decided at that time to change and be on his side, and I asked him to reduce the tension a bit: - Mr. Ospina, can I ask you a question by chance? -As a non-countryman, you can ask me any question you want -and he repeated the word countryman as if to tell us: "I'm Cuban too". Eaten by curiosity, I asked Alfonso: - Sir, what do those pictures that he has put all over the walls of his office say?

- That's the disadvantage of not speaking more than one language - he replied with some vanity: -That's an inscription in the Aramaic language and he says verbatim: I'm watching you. - And he added: - I like your curiosity and I'm going to be understanding and also splendid with you, and I'm going to offer you a good deal. -

- What deal is the countryman going to offer us? I asked him.

Alfonso answered me: - I offer you the same thing that Henry offered you. You guys go back to Miami and tell Henry that I hid, and they couldn't find me, that's totally understandable in a city of over 23 million people. Go into that office next to this one, which is a conference room, sit quietly, speak quietly and without much gesturing, and consider my offer. I am going to wait for you here for a few minutes and if you accept what I have proposed, I am not going to have to stain my hands with blood, with the blood of my countrymen, because, although it may not seem like it, I am also like you. , Cuban. Although I grew up here in this concrete jungle, I was born in Havana in the Jesús María neighborhood. So guys, please come to the conference room and think very carefully about what is best for you to do at this time.

- I understood that it was not convenient for us to continue arguing with that powerful and intelligent individual and I told my companions. - Guys, let's go to the room to deliberate. Alfonso told me: - I see that you are beginning to reason and I like that. I think they are smart and brave, although they can be too brave or half crazy, but they have material for this business. In a different situation I would have offered to work with me. After saying this he made a hand signal for us to enter the room.

- That guy created me a piece of furniture to have good wood. I ignored Aracel's stupidity and didn't answer him, but I took the floor: - Gentlemen, we are dead and we stink like a corpse, because we don't have the slightest chance of winning this game, because as you can understand this is simply a trap. This guy is already waiting for us with everything well set up and among Henry's people there is more than one spy, when it's not Henry himself and from what I see between Henry and Alfonso, they want us as a scapegoat. We are going to accept what Alfonso is offering us and let's get out of here as soon as possible, because Alfonso's tooth of a church pastor and national solidarity, I don't believe it. Here's something else, but to find out we have to get out of here alive and kicking, and not in a concrete column as Brother Alfonso has offered us. -

- It could be that the same spy is Henry - the fat Aracel told me - because it seems to me that the real owners of the splinter are the two Barranquilleros, otherwise why did Henry take them to the restaurant La Perla del Mar, the afternoon in what do we go out? -How did he say his name is him?

- I took the floor: - Yes, that so-called Salim had to see our faces for Henry to discharge the responsibility of collecting the money on us. And now we are not going to talk any more here, because as Alfonso himself told me, here the walls have eyes and ears, and remember what the happy little square says, they are watching us. -

- Indeed Aracel the fat man was very right and Alfonso was listening to our entire conversation. Then I found out that taking Salim and Pacho to meet us, the one who cost him his life was Henry, but I will tell you about that story later.

"But that sounds more like a police novel than reality," Lázaro told Silvio.

- Don't worry, partner, this is missing the best -and he added a poem to the story-: I ask silence and silence to pay attention, I'm going this time if my memory helps me show you that my story was missing the best.

- You're made a poet. Where did you get the poetry? Lázaro asked.

-From a book of poetry, from an Argentine poet, the great José Hernández from his immortal work Martín Fierro.

- You are cultivating a lot of peasants - Lázaro told him.

- Let me continue my story, because when the plane arrives, we are going to be halfway though.

- Not at all, cute - Lázaro replied - if it's not here it's in Miami, but you just told me the story.

"Let me continue," he said to Lázaro and continued: "With everyone in agreement, we returned to that spacious office from where you could admire the greatness of the city of New York, for me the city of traps."

- Again I took the floor: - Well, Mr. Ospina, my friends and I have agreed... Alfonso did not let me finish my sentence: - I know that you have decided to take the money that I offer you and return to Miami to enjoy the sun and tell Henry that you haven't seen my face. Isn't that what you wanted to tell me? -

- In effect, that is our decision, - I told Alfonsito. And he answered me: - You have acted with great sanity and you have managed to convince your friends and even if you don't believe it you have saved their lives and you have saved yourself. - Of course we believe you Mr. Alfonso - answered Julito.

- Alfonso picked up the phone and spoke authoritatively: - Manuel, please come to my office. -In a few minutes a side door opened and a dark giant entered and in perfect Spanish, he asked: -Tell me, Mr. Ospina, what am I good for? - By the tone of voice the gigantic brunette was Colombian.

- Accompany these gentlemen to the basement of the building and deliver what we have prepared for them. - My hair stood on end again. "What we have prepared for them" sounded more like cement to me than money. Lázaro, I swear to you that if the pistols had had real bullets, it would have ended like a guatao party, but there was nothing I could do, I restrained myself and left everything in the hands of God or my destiny. I understood that if they were already expecting us, they had to have some plan laid out for us beforehand.

-Before saying goodbye to Alfonso, he told us: -Guys, there is a small problem with the money, because it is in low-denomination bills. It's on $5, $10, and $1 bills. Do you have no objection? - For our part none, - I replied - it is money and as you say it is worth the same and it is also proof that there is no counterfeit bill.

- The black man made a signal with his hand to follow him and the four of us took the supersonic elevator in that building. And in a few minutes we were in the basement of the building, where 10 or 12 Alfonso's henchmen were waiting for us, also armed to the teeth. My hair stood on end again and I saw myself at the bottom of the Hudson River melted into a concrete block and sunk into the mud of the river bed. I looked at my companions for a moment and noticed that they were just as scared as I was. I pretended to be strong so as not to scare them anymore. -

- To my surprise, Alfonso's men gave us three cloth worm bags full of 10, 5 and 1 dollar bills, and we, without the slightest concern (and pure innocence) let ourselves take a movie carrying the bags full of bills and putting them in the trunk of the brand new white Monte Carlo. -

- And how did they get out of the building? Lázaro asked.

- Imagine you, we came out like the dog that knocked over the can. And already on the way back on the New Jersey Turnpike, they put our testicles back in place, because until that moment we had it in our mouths -

- Aracel spoke, with a lump in her voice: - We have escaped for good and the best thing is that with money. - I answered them, with my throat almost dry from the nerves that we had gone through: - Now we are out of a problem with Alfonso Ospina, but we have another one with Henry. How about he doesn't believe the story that we didn't find his man.

- But that's what we're going to tell Henry? Julito asked. - That is what we are going to tell him, that he is going to believe us, it is another 20 pesos. -

- In less than 24 hours we arrived in Miami and went through our humble house to leave the hidden money. Then we went to El Quisqueya to face Henry. As we got closer to the destination, the silence inside the vehicle became more dense. The 3 of us were terrified, about to lie to a ruthless murderous mobster. We entered the bar and Henry was waiting for us leaning against the bar, accompanied by the two men from Barranquilla, Salim and Pacho Murillo, and at least 5 more hit men, all armed, as always. Henry from the bar waved us out. - How's my troop? How was he on the trip? I suppose that they were successful in the management that I entrusted to them. I hope so, it gives me a hunch. -

-I answered him what he had practiced in my mind all the way, verbatim words, studied: -Well, this time your hunch failed him, because we have miserably wasted time. We couldn't see anyone, or photos; it seems that Alfonso was swallowed up by the earth, it is such a big city and with so many people it is very difficult to find someone who wants to hide. Apparently someone warned him of our arrival and that gave him time to hide. -

- Do you want to tell me that among us there is a snitch, a traitor? Henry said with a scowling face. - I don't want to tell you anything, - I replied - I can only tell you that someone gave you notice of our arrival. But Henry was an Indian who had the wickedness of a white man and the Indian did not want to take any risk: - Okay, this time we have not been lucky, it will be another time, but for now I need my pistols and car keys back. . And he told one of his henchmen: - Rafael picks up the three pistols and the car key that the boys are going to give you. -Rafael proceeded with diligence to carry out the order of his boss, knowing that this action at the end of the day would make his job as a bully with us easier.

- We had no choice but to deliver the weapons and be supposedly unarmed.

Lázaro asked him: - And why supposedly unarmed? -

- I'll tell you. -Silvio answered- As I told you, we were supposedly left unarmed at the mercy of Henry and his henchmen, who told us: - It's a pity that they didn't find Alfonso, but don't lose hope it will be again. Now I want you to see something that will interest you. -

During that talk with Henry, neither Salim nor Pacho had opened their mouths. They concentrated on observing everything thoroughly, with a face of doubt about everything and everyone. I think the one who gave him the most confidence was Henry, it may be that Aracel el Gordo's deduction was correct.

-But come on guys -Henry told us-, come to the bar office I want you to see a movie that Alfonso sent me from New York by DHL and since he came by plane he arrived before you. -

- I immediately understood that we were in trouble. We entered the office of the bar, Henry, Pacho, Salím and the three of us. The group of assassins stayed outside waiting for what they already knew would happen. Henry took the beta cassette out of a small desk where Pedro, the Dominican, did the bills for the bar and placed it in a player next to a small television and told us: - Guys, look at the movie Alfonso sent me. How interesting is your film, visiting Mr. Alfonso's office in New York City, the city where you couldn't find him because one of my men gave you notice of his arrival. -

- There, in that movie, the three of us were carrying the olive green packages with $10, $5, $1 bills. -

- Where's my two million? Henry asked as he banged on the table. His face filled with fury. The Murillo brothers, unmoved, looked at us waiting for an answer.

Julito replied: -The only thing that guy gave us was 500,000 dollars -

Then I began to understand the trap. Henry owed Murillo that money and had found 3 assholes that gave him the perfect excuse not to pay it back. With Alfonso in New York they devised the illusion that they were given the 2 million but in reality it was much less. The video was evidence that they paid and the thieves decided to steal it. Case closed.

- Henry shouted: - How so? Do you want to make me stupid? Do you want me to believe that between three tulas there was only $500,000? Are you trying to make fun of me? And he repeated in a more violent tone, hitting the table again: Where is my money? -

One of the gunmen, hearing the commotion, came through the door and pointed his gun at Julito's head.

- Don't kill us, it's the truth - Julito said between sobs. - They gave us all small bills, pesos, $5, $10 and $20. There were a lot of bills, but little money. -

Those who recorded the video positioned themselves from afar, so as not to show the numbers on the bills. It was part of the macabre plan.

- Did you see my stupid face? Henry yelled. He was a good actor, playing the role of a victim ripped off by a couple of unscrupulous crooks. He was actually condemning 3 starving innocents to die.

-If my partner in New York tells me that he gave you the 2 million dollars, who do you think I'm going to believe?

The assassin drew the hammer of his revolver back, as if preparing to shoot. The sound penetrated the bones of the 3 Cubans. There was a soft cry, a deep wail.

- I have them - I answered terrified. - I have the money and I can take you where you are. -My plan B was in motion, one that he had thought of during the long hours of returning to Miami. I had not told my 2 partners because I was afraid that they would be frightened, because they were convinced that the lie was going to work and I did not want to create any doubts. The only option at that time was to lie to get out of the mess, we had never analyzed that scenario together. I wanted to get out of that place alive as soon as possible and that's why I played my last card: lie so as not to die.

- So my two million that my friend Alfonso Ospina sent me with you 3 and that you have wanted to play with me, Silvio has. - The capo asked me for the third time, now a little calmer: - Where is my money? -

- I replied: - Yes sir, I have it hidden. The ambition of the money was painted on the face of Henry, who knew that there were not 2 million dollars in those sacks, but at least he would recover the half million that we brought from New York. Then he said, "Okay, then go get them and bring it to me right now." - And turning to Pacho and Salím, he told them: - Haven't they told you that Alfonso Ospina is a man of his word?

- Let's wait for the talk to appear to make deductions - answered Salim, with a face of not believing anything of that comedy that Henry and Alfonso had put together taking us as an instrument.

- You're going to be accompanied by one of my men - repeated Henry and added: - Everyone stays here to wait for the money and if he's not back in an hour I'll give both of them a flat. -

Fear wouldn't let me think clearly, but suddenly I realized that only I was going to get out of that place alive. I was leaving behind my 2 lifelong friends, my cronies, those of us who came to this land of freedom to achieve our dreams. But now we were living a nightmare, a horrible nightmare, and the only thing on my mind was to survive. When I left that office I looked at them, asking for forgiveness with my eyes but hiding my pain so as not to give away my plan. It was the last time I saw them in my life. -

- We left the office and addressing one of his assassins, the same one who had disarmed us, ordered him: - Rafael accompanies this pelao to collect the money that my friend Alfonso sent me with them, and if he wants to be brave or

He wants to be smart, you give me the low and you bring me the head here. -

- The hitman waved me out of the bar and we went to the white Monte Carlo. As I sat down on the helm side, Henry's thug sat down next to me and opened his shirt to reveal a gun he had on his waistband. What that man did not know and now you will understand why he had told you that I was not totally unarmed, was that he carried a small 25mm caliber pistol in his pants pocket, with a bullet in the direct-

Lázaro interrupted Silvio and asked: - Do you now bring that weapon here in the boat?

Silvio replied: - Of course not, my brother, I know that one of your rules is not to bring firearms on the boat, I am very respectful of that, and you are my friends.

- It's good that you know that, no firearms, no drinks, no drugs - said Lázaro and added: - In a fast rattling boat, a firearm is only good to give you 5 more years of sentence.

- You know Lázaro that I'm not violent, nor do I like blood and I've been in this business more because I'm lazy than because I'm handsome, and I carry my little pistol because it saved my life the time the Jamaicans tried to knock me down. But at that moment the only chance to escape alive was my little pistol, do you understand me? -

Lázaro nodded, but with a very intrigued face.

- In the one driven by 27th Street to the south I was scheming, looking for the best way out of that hole. I thought about getting to the light and shooting the hitman, shooting the animal that was with me in the head and running out of the car, going back to the bar and rescuing my companions. In the end, that car was not in my name. Although I liked the idea, it annoyed me to stain my hands with the rotten blood of that contract killer and, worse still, to stain a cream-colored Monte Carlos seat. I walked down 22nd Avenue and on First Street I remembered that a police station had just opened. Then I saw the heavens open and, more than anything, the possibility of not having to kill anyone. I stopped at the intersection, and when they put the green light I entered the parking lot of the police station and told the hitman: - Your boss's money is here, in this place. - I got out of the vehicle with the keys in my hand and like lightning I entered the Miami police building.

"You put it on him in China," Lázaro commented, his eyes wide open. Silvio smiled nervously and continued the story.

- The hitman was completely frozen without knowing what to do. It was not logical that he would attack me there in front of a police station, because the most handsome plays with the chain, but not with the monkey, and you know that in Miami the police do not play, if he had fired the slightest shot they would break him in two.

I stared out the window to see his reaction. He looked around a bit with a panic face, got out of the car and left that place as fast as possible. Perhaps he imagined that I was going to report him and 10 police officers would run out, guns drawn, to arrest him. I don't think he would have done very well.

- You disconcerted him - said Lázaro. - What a great plan you came up with at that time. -

- So it was, I completely baffled him. I imagine that the human mind, under such pressure, in the face of imminent death, becomes very creative. - Silvio said a little more relaxed. - See if my creativity had been activated to the maximum and inside the building I had to justify my presence there, armed, without raising suspicion. So I went in front of the officer who was behind the window, and I told him: - Officer, I found this gun on the street. I understand from the propaganda I've seen on TV that you guys give $100 reward for each weapon that remains out of the hands of a criminal. - I took out the gun very carefully to prevent him from feeling threatened and I showed it to him. -

- For a brief moment it crossed my mind to tell the officer that two of my friends were in danger very close by, but my instinct screamed inside me that, if I did that, I was condemning myself to a long stay in jail. Again, survival betrayed me. Today I think I should have done it, but I can't turn back time anymore. -

- Yes - the officer told me - you are right, citizen. The policeman took the gun, put it in a nylon, gave me a form, and told me: - Fill out this form and within 6 to 8 weeks you will receive a check for $100 dollars and a letter of congratulations from high to crime.

- While I was filling out the form, I looked out the window of the building and saw the Monte Carlo parked and I imagined the hit man returning to the Quisqueya to tell Henry what had happened. Or maybe not, maybe he ran to the airport to return to Colombia instead of having to admit to a dangerous narco that a man valued at 2 million dollars had escaped him.

 - Weren't you worried that your friends told Henry, under torture, that the money was in the efficiency where they lived? Lázaro said.

- Yes, I knew I had to hurry back to the house and get him out of there but first I had to finish my charade at the police station. He didn't know if the hitman called his boss on the phone to tell her the news or if he had left on foot to say it in person. I also didn't know how long it would take for my friends to confess. -

"You left them stuck in a tremendous fire," Lázaro commented.

- Of course, partner, I had no choice but to make a nice tombstone for my friends because not even the Chinese doctor could save them. - Silvio reflected with nostalgia in his gaze.

- I really thought of poor Julito, the paisa, and Aracel, the fat one, and I felt sorry, but human beings are selfish and much more when it comes to facing death or distributing money, but I'm sure that if I would have stayed anyway they would kill the three of us and no one would have stayed to tell the story. Because it was going to be impossible to convince them that we didn't steal the money. We only had half a million and Henry would never have let the Murillo brothers know that everything had been a deception devised by Alfonso and him to steal 2 million from the Barranquilla drug traffickers. -

- I quickly left the police station and went to our house to get the money. I knew my minutes were numbered. I imagined that Aracel and Julito were going to resist as long as possible before handing over the loot, in the hope that they could negotiate with the Colombians and leave them alive. Luckily when I got to the building everything seemed normal and I was able to get the bags out without any problem. With no apparent direction, I started driving north, the only possible option to leave the state of Florida. -

- Suddenly a thought came to my mind that felt like a bucket of ice water. The Monte Carlo! I couldn't keep driving that car, it was hot. Colombians could call 911 and say that I was armed and that I had drug money in the trunk to throw the police on me. Maybe it was stolen, I had never seen the papers for that car. So I decided that if I was going to run away I had to buy another vehicle, and money was not an issue. -

- I left the Monte Carlo parked and locked up on a street in downtown Miami, on 8th Street, and with $10,000 in hand I went into a car dealer that I saw on the way. I asked the salesman what was the strongest and most durable car he had, ideal for traveling on the road. And after showing me several, he sold me a white Ford Mustang Cobra with blue stripes that ran all the way from the hood to the trunk. It wasn't the most economical or the one that saved the most gasoline, but I always wanted to have a car like that, since I lived in Cuba. I signed the papers, they gave me the title and I quickly went out to see if the Montecarlo was still stopped where I left it, always thinking that the police might be looking for me. -

- And you found it? - Lázaro inquired very interested in the story.

- Yeah, breathe a sigh of relief. I parked behind it, took the tulas with the money out of the trunk and put them in the Mustang. Before starting I felt, for the first time, the sensation that everything was going well, and I prayed to myself that Aracel and Julito were alive. Silvio commented with an air of sadness.

"But it wasn't like that," Lázaro said, with a bit of resentment in his voice.

- You are not right. Three days later my friends were found dead in the trunk of a stolen car. They had been beaten to death after being tortured. A week later and with half a million dollars, tax free to spend, I arrived in the city of San Diego, California. -

- No, you never found out if they went to the apartment to get the money, if they confessed? - Lázaro asked.

- No, I thought I'd call a neighbor to find out but...

A distorted voice on the speaker interrupted the story.

- Master, master, master, this is Silver Eagle. -Silvio ran, took the two-meter radius in his hand and replied: -Go ahead silver eagle, here teacher, I'm in position.-

Yoel and Jairo ran onto the cabin of the boat and jumped down next to us. Yoel took the helm of the boat, started the engines, and the four men saw that black, Dantesque bird appear in the twilight of the Caribbean afternoon, flying over the sea, making the two engines roar.

After the tremendous story that he had just heard, Lázaro felt, suddenly, that he returned his soul to his body. There he realized that he was doing what he likes the most. He always felt that this bombing operation, of throwing the cargo into the sea and then floating it up, is the most exciting of a smuggling operation, because it involves the entire navy, air force and men on the ground. True to his motto: "I like to live dangerously" he felt his veins fill with adrenaline and an instinct, a mixture of danger and emotion, took over his body.

Silvio lit a small lantern that he had in his briefcase, a maneuver taken from the best maritime drug trafficker's manual. It is used to prevent one of those huge packages from falling on the boat and sinking it, or hurting any of the crew. A missile weighing 40 to 50 pounds, falling from 500 feet, launched from an aircraft coming at 200 kilometers per hour, it is logical to assume that it can cause havoc.

DC3 similar to the one used by Colombian smugglers to move drugs

The DC3 flew over the crew for the second time and the first thing it threw into the water was the empty fuel bladder, since the distance of the trip meant that the pilots were always forced to carry extra fuel. They left from Aruba or Curaçao and from there they had to fly to the Colombian Guajira Peninsula where they picked up the cargo. They then set course for the Bahama Islands passing through Haiti, for a total distance of 1,200 miles.

For this reason, these planes always carried a large amount of extra fuel that allowed them to refuel in mid-flight.

The plane flew low over the ship and suddenly a unique spectacle occurred before the astonished gaze of those present: the line of green lights began to fall like emerald boots in the ocean, and the noise of packages crashing against the waves broke the silence of the night. Just as it came as a surprise, the DC3 disappeared into the darkness that was already taking over the afternoon. And the beautiful Caribbean twilight gave way to night.

But no beautiful scenery was going to distract these smugglers. It was time to get to work.

Yoel sat down at the helm and Lázaro took the boat hook in his hands like a painter takes a brush, ready to do what he knows best. Silvio and Jairo got ready to help get the packages out of the water.

The boat approached the first green light that was about 50 meters away. A string attached it to a black canvas bag, inside which was a package of 20 to 25 kilos of marijuana.

Luckily that night the sea was calm, with little waves and the bank of the Bahamas was completely calm. Lázaro remembered the times that he had to pick up 50 packages with waves up to five or six feet high (between 1.5 and 2 meters).

Lázaro hooked the first package and pulled it towards the boat. With the help of his comrades he managed to get him into the boat.

He looked at Silvio and told him: - Arrange them all in the cabin, but you have to place them well. Cover all the spaces, put the briefcases and the life preservers next to the anchor, we need everything to fit in. Remember that later we have to pick up the Murillo brothers' sailboat, because if we don't do that job, our friend Jairo doesn't get paid.

- What Lázaro says is so - said the boy, who was helping them with great enthusiasm - My wife is waiting for me in Miami to change the car for a new one. You know, compadre, how women spend the money that one earns with so much risk and sacrifice.

"It's the law of life, brother," answered Yoel, who was also called the Arrow, from the helm of the Mirage.

- It's okay - Silvio replied to Lázaro and added: - I'm going to try to do my best, remember that I'm not a boatman and I don't have much practice in that kind of work.

Jairo cut one of the strings, picked up the package and went to throw the light into the sea.

- Waiting! Do not do that! Lázaro shouted urgently.

It was evident that the Colombian had zero experience in collecting merchandise from the sea. He stopped in time and looked at Lázaro, confused.

- You don't have the lights in the sea, throw them in that bucket that is here, because if you throw lights in the sea, we won't know which ones are packages with lights and which lights have nothing and we would go crazy, we would waste a lot of time.

- You're quite right. - Jairo replied.

Silvio supported him saying:

-He has something more than reason, he also has the experience that we don't have, and also as the Greek sage said...

Silvio was distracted when he saw a green light in the distance.

- And what did the Greek sage say? Jairus asked.

- Zapatero to your shoe, everyone to their own and every job has its trick.

The phrase "Shoemaker to your shoe" is attributed to a 1st century Greek painter named Apelles, one of whose paintings was criticized by a shoemaker. Offended, he told her "Ne sutor ultra crepidam", the Latin equivalent of the famous phrase.

Yoel took the floor:-Apparently Silvio has been doing something more than playing roosters lately, he has been reading. -

Silvio barely had time to smile because the ship had come close enough to another of the bundles for him to reach it.

They repeated this work for 2 hours and managed to get 56 packages out of the sea. Silvio did a good job in the cabin and took up half of it. Yoel asked him:

- How many packages did your plane drop? -

- 56 packages, - Sílvio replied - and they are all placed in the cabin, we have worked as professionals and leave room for the next load. -

- Of those 56 packages, 14 are from us. Yoel said.

- No my brother, there are only 11 of you, remember that we adjusted 20%, don't hit me against the wall. Silvio said with concern.

- It is not good that these children learn so much. - Lázaro replied and added, smiling: - They can try to take our job away from us. -

- I don't think anyone wants to take this type of work away from them. It is very hard and dangerous, I am a man of the land and not of the sea, and only tonight I am here with you just for the sake of survival.

- Well, guys, if we're done here, hang on because I'm going to look for the Murillo brothers' sailboat.

They took off like a rocket to the east, in the direction of the tongue lighthouse. The night was dark; the moon, in a waning quarter, favors the navigators, who traveled with all the lights off, only the compass and the engine clocks turned on.

Yoell kept a close eye on the compass, the temperature gauges, the ammeter, and the tachometer that measures the engine's revolutions. The lights on the engine console were covered with a coat, because on a dark night at sea, the slightest light is seen far away.

The 36-foot Mirage boat with two 330-horsepower engines, manufactured by the old Conte, the one from Batabanó, flew over the waters of the Bahamas bank and in less than an hour and a half they were in the meeting with the sailboat.

They decided not to drop anchor here either, especially now that they were loaded and in that circumstance it is not advisable to anchor, because nobody knows if they are going to have to run in an area patrolled by the Bahamian Defense Forces or by the helicopter of the gringo coast guard In addition, that place was very close to the Nassau airport, and as Yoel said: - Look at the rascal, we are in the way of everyone who goes to Florida. -

Yoel asked Jairo: - Was it just this place that your people had to choose to deliver the work to us? -

The Colombian shrugged his shoulders as if to say: "I don't rule here, I only obey."

Already around 9 at night and as was his custom, Yoel sat on the bow of the boat on the cabin to fish, accompanied by Jairo. Silvio and Lázaro continued talking about the subject that had been interrupted by the arrival of the plane.

- I arrived in California, in the city of San Diego, on the border with Mexico, and with the money I had brought I did several businesses and none of them turned out well. As the saying goes: "What was bad, the devil takes it", because I lost everything. I'll be honest, I also lost a lot of money on occasional visits to the city of Las Vegas, the gaming capital of the world. I was, as they say in Cuba, completely stunned, and unable to return to Florida, because I knew nothing of Henry's death. I thought that he and his henchmen were looking for me, and for fear of running into the Colombians, I had no choice but to stay there and start inventing. During the time I was traveling through California and Mexico I found very good friends, and I tell you, if this works out for me, I may return to California, because I know that with money I can do business there. -

Henry was shot to death after he returned to Cali, Colombia, his hometown. Other drug traffickers say that he had given his wife $500,000 to keep them. One day he returned to his house, knocked on the door but the woman did not open it. He kept hitting, insisting without success. Suddenly, 2 men appeared who were waiting for him hidden and shot him 6 times. Many say that the wife had him killed to keep the money. the crime was never investigated by the Colombian authorities.

- With money you can do business anywhere in the world. Lázaro said.

They both smiled knowingly. Money was something that united them, "quick money, but not easy", something they never tired of repeating. Drug traffickers don't usually think about anything else, only money, pleasures, the good life. The rest is too depressing.

Silvio asked Lázaro: - Do you think you're going there with me? -

Lázaro hesitated to answer. - No, partner, we are from salt water and not from land, but when the time comes and according to the reward, we will see what can be done. -

Silvio told Lázaro that on her pilgrimage through Mexico he had met a girl from the city of Hermosillo, in the state of Sonora, and that he had had a relationship with her. And that he had been the father of a girl named Carolina. This girl was a relative of one of the capos of Northern Mexico.

- Those people work hard, but they are very dangerous and violent people and I am a man of peace. - Lázaro hastened to say.

- There is no problem in that - Silvio said with a tone that inferred confidence - you in contact with me and I in contact with them, they have me in the middle and there is nothing to worry about.

- So it may be fine because I have no interest in having a problem with them - Lázaro replied. - You know that we do not bring any firearms on the boat and we say, as the bearded man said in one of his first lies, "weapons for what?", and then he brought so much Russian weapons into the country that it almost sank Cuba . -

- It almost sinks, it is not fair to say. Fair enough to say he sank it. Silvio added.

They continued chatting animatedly, until Lázaro asked him:

- Partner, what time does your watch have?

It was Yoel the arrow who answered:

-It's 12 o'clock at night, that sailboat must have been here, he may have had problems on the Island of San Andrés or he may also have been imprisoned. We can't wait for more than half past twelve.

- We have to wait at least until 2 in the morning - said Jairo, with a voice of concern.

"At half past twelve we're leaving, not a minute more," Lázaro said, supporting his partner.

- Guys, if that sailboat doesn't arrive I won't make any money - replied the Colombian, already a little more nervous.

- We are very sorry for you and the Murillo family, but we are not responsible for this delay - answered Yoel and told him: - But calm down because if that thing on the bow reaches the crown, you will have your 20 lucas safe in your hands, courtesy of Trampin Company, money that you have already earned with the help you have given to the director of Trampin Company.

- I think that the Arrow has made a mistake, because the correct thing to say is General Director Yoel - Lázaro replied.

"I understand now because the boss always gives him more time," Silvio told him.

While the Cubans laughed, more than anything to ease the tension of the moment, the Colombian suffered from the delay of the sailboat, Jairo gave the talk a serious touch:

- What you have told me that you are going to share with me reassures me, because not everyone does that. And what happened Jairo with your work as a painter? Because Jairo Fernando Murillo had told me that you were working as a painter and that you were doing very well, and that you knew how to do the job very well.

- I don't think the work of a painter is less hard than this, which is not easy at all - Lázaro told him.

- That is very loose, sometimes the paintings are sold and sometimes not. Do you think that if I sold the paintings and gave me enough money to have my family, I would be here risking my life and freedom? I don't have a vocation as a smuggler - answered the Colombian thinking that Lázaro was a talented painter. He actually painted walls.

- And do you think that we do have that vocation? Lázaro told him.

- This work for me is not a crime, this work for me is an adventure - Yoel told them.

- What a pity that the others and mainly the law do not have the same opinion, and if they catch us playing the role of The Black Corsair, Emilio Salgari plays The Count of Monte Cristo by Alexandre Dumas, they are going to put us a ball of years in prison - Lázaro said.

-He who is afraid of dogs, he cannot be a postman-said Silvio, and reminded Jairo:-At 12:30 we leave. -

The gaze of the four men was fixed on the east, where the Murillo brothers' sailboat was supposed to appear, but it would never arrive. At 12:30 p.m. the order was given to leave "throwing whores" or, how could it also be said colloquially: "burning tennis."

- Gentlemen, are we going now? Jairus asked.

- Bugle bugle - answered Lázaro and added: - I think his wife's new cart was screwed up, but don't complain any more than we've already told you that, if everything is fine, you take what's yours in your pocket, if not it's because Silvio shows up, we would all have left with the ball of rags.

- You are right, we would all have left with the ball of the rag, - Jairo said - because I'm thinking that Murillo's sailboat fell in combat, poor sailors who came on it. I know three of them, they are from my town and they are newlyweds and now they are going to be away from his wife and his family for years and especially from his mother, who is the one who really suffers. But come on, the sailboat doesn't really come and we still don't know if it's for our good or for our bad.

Yoel started the Mirage's engines, and the ship sped west toward the Florida coast. The sea was calm. The 2,200 pounds that the silver eagle had bombarded them with had a value at that time of $1,100,000, at a rate of $500 per pound, of which 20% was for the boatmen. 5% for Silvio and the rest for the owners of the merchandise, the Murillo brothers.

- Yoel turns on the navigation lights while we are on the bank, Jairo watches the rear, I to starboard and you, Silvio, to port and open your eyes wide that the patrol boat Gran Inagua is prowling around the area, as my old mother told me. And I don't want to have to run, I don't want to sleep on Fort Hill in Nassau tonight.

- And what is Fort Hill? Silvio asked Lázaro.

- You don't want to know that ugly place, because I haven't been there, but I've been told that it's very unpleasant, and if the blacks surprise us, you're going to spend a good time there, with a good kick in the ass. Fort Hill is the prison of the Bahamas Islands and is in Nassau. -

"Then I am going to be very careful not to have to collide with the enemy tonight," said Jairo.

And Lázaro, the group's philosopher, replied: - No Jairo, the enemy is not the black Bahamians, our true enemy is fear.

- You're absolutely right, - answered the Colombian - nerves are what almost always betray us.

The Mirage continued to steam west with her crew and her cargo. Lázaro warned the Arrow: - Don't stick to the island, remember what the black mother told us, we are going to take this precaution and enter the channel between the sunken ship and Cayó del Gato, we will navigate there for an hour and please everyone on close watch.

- I have the sunken ship in the boat test, but I don't see the masthead lights of any vessel next to the sunken ship -the Arrow answered-, I am seeing the helicopter flying over Cayo del Gato. I'm going to turn off the lights on the console. Take out the Blue tarpaulin in case the helicopter comes over us, cover ourselves with it so that it can serve as camouflage. -

The disadvantage, at that moment, was that the night was very dark. After unfolding the tarp over the boat, they sat quietly for an hour without making a sound. Time was pressing and they couldn't wait any longer, and there was still a big surprise waiting for them off the coast of Florida.

"It seems to me that the helicopter has already left," said the Arrow to his companions after a time that seemed a lot like eternity.

Lázaro gave him instructions again: - Pick up the canvas and put the engines on low, we are going to sail slowly, only with the navigation lights on to confuse you as if we were a yacht sailing from Nassau to Miami.

"We have some lights on the right," Jairo warned them.

- I think they are rich people fishing on a yacht for lamb. They go trolling, because the yacht moves very slowly. As an old sailor would say, they go with black sails.

The launch reached the edge of the channel and everyone was scanning the horizon like cats trying to see in the dark of night.

The Arrow saw a sign of danger and told them: - I'm seeing in the distance a rigging of a ship that I don't like, it could be the American Coast Guard.

- If it is the coast guard that we saw a while ago, it is heading south, surely towards the bank of Cayo Sal. Let it go away, as my mother used to say, "take it, wind of water". We can't waste any more time or we're going to have to go into the daylight slot, and if that happens, we're toast. We are going to have to leave, as a Puerto Rican would say: "on fire". -

Lázaro said, with a disguised tone of confidence: - Leather the horse and may providence assist us. -

They entered La Canal, the space of sea that separated the Bahama Islands from the Florida Peninsula, called by them that way because the Gulf Stream ran through it, a water current that is born in the Caribbean Sea and, after crossing the Atlantic Ocean, reaches England, warming cold Britain.

- The moment of truth has arrived, it's time to kill the cigar or be killed by it, - Lázaro sentenced and added - don't fall asleep and watch closely so that the tie we saw sailing south doesn't surprise us. -

The Flecha headed for Miami 270° on the compass and Silvio asked him: - Isn't it towards the Keys where we have to sail? Isn't that where you have the gap between the millionaires' club and Cayo Largo?

- If what you say is correct, it is along the old highway of the keys, between the millionaires' club and Cayo Largo. -

- Then why are we sailing to Miami? - Silvio asked him.

- Very good observation - Lázaro told him who was listening to the conversation and asked Silvio: - And if you're not a sailor, how do you know that we're heading to Miami?

- Well, I'm not a sailor, but I'm not that rough either and I'm seeing in the compass 270° that it is straight west, if we were heading towards Cayo Largo, I would have put 240° in the compass, besides if we were heading for Miami it's time that we were seeing the claret of the city.

Silvio's face showed more arrogance than concern. He had no doubt done this route before but he refused to admit it. Lázaro knew that no one knows degrees or directions without having studied or lived it. And Silvio had a studious face, he didn't have one.

- But as you yourself have said, you are from the land and we are from the sea and we know how to do our job well - Lázaro explained to Silvio.

- In fact, we crossed the channel from Bimini to Miami, we do it as a strategy to disorient the government radars, because if the radar detects us doing this course, the authorities assume that it is a fishing boat that is returning from the Bahamas. Making or setting course for the Keys directly becomes more suspicious, that course is part of a strategy, and then along the coast we set course south and sail parallel to it. Lázaro explained with the face of a professor, a performance that he had practiced for a long time in front of his students in the history class.

Little by little, the lights of the airport's communications towers faded away while the entire glow of the city of Miami appeared to the west. They only bumped into three merchant ships during the trip, including a gigantic tanker that made them feel like ants next to an elephant. The claret was already getting bigger and the first red dots of lights appeared that, by law, buildings have to carry on their chests. During the crossing, the sea had been calm, but already at dawn it was beginning to rise.

After passing Fowey Rocks, an in-water lighthouse south of Key Biscayne, Arrow headed south 180° on the compass toward Key Largo, Monroe County's northernmost key. The whole group was in maximum tension, that area of the sea is closely guarded by American patrols and none of them wanted to lose that bet, they bet not only on money, but also on the most important thing for a man, they bet on freedom and life.

Heading towards the Keys, they passed by the small Triunfo Lighthouse and then by the tallest Atlantic lighthouse to continue south, until they passed by the Berreona buoy, which indicates the entrance to the Bay of Millionaires.

Already passing by the buoy they saw the Cary Fort forum flash on their left, two flashes every 30 seconds. The moment of truth had arrived. Then they headed 200° with the engines at low revolutions, and with the wet exhausts very silent, they advanced towards the famous "hole of the moored ones".

That is a small entrance in the mangrove, used sometimes by merry fishermen and lobstermen and other times by smugglers. The place communicates with the old highway of the Keys, which begins in Florida City and ends at the entrance to Key Largo.

The "hollow of the moorings' connects the sea through a trio or path between the mangrove with the old highway of the Keys. The path is so narrow that it only allows the passage of one vehicle. It is only half a mile long through the trees, and it is so dark at night that it is impossible to see your hands. Raccoons and snakes abound in this mangrove swamp, which is now a Florida state animal and plant sanctuary.

Arriving there, the boatmen faced the United States Coast Guard, the customs service, the Border Service, the maritime patrol, the animal life conservation patrol, the local police and if this were not enough , to the tumbadores, that is, the thieves who steal from traffickers.

Yoel and Lázaro assumed that Manolo and Rosendo, their accomplices on the ground, had already taken up a position in the area and placed a man with a radio at the entrance to the trail with the mission of sounding the alarm or warning of any unexpected visit or inopportune And that they also had a truck ready to transport the drug to Miami.

The Murillos brothers had received the bad news that the sailboat had had technical problems on the Colombian island of San Andrés, and would not arrive at the planned location on time that night. And they had told Manolo and Rosendo not to go wait in the hole, and that way they wouldn't have to suffer from the annoying mosquitoes and the bad night. Therefore, neither Manolo nor Rosendo had gone to wait for them, they had stayed at home, in the warmth of their wives and snoring like locomotives.

The boat arrived in front of the "hollow of the moored" and Yoel stopped the engines so that inertia would transport them the last few meters. It was evident that they were totally alone in unloading the 56 packages. The four men with their nerves on edge and adrenaline on the surface tried to see the owls around them. The launch approached the shore with the slowness of a tiger approaching its prey. But in this case the dam could hide 100 federal agents ready to learn from them.

- Brother, give the agreed signal to Manolo. We are now less than 100 meters from the nose of the canal entrance. -

Lázaro took a small matchbox out of his pants pocket and clicked it two or three times. The stone gave off sparks that lit up the night.

And everyone, with a deathly silence, waited for an answer. It must have been the same, three sparks from Manolo's or Rosendo's matchbox.

Any.

El Flecha told Lázaro: - Our people aren't in the hole, neither Manolo nor Rosendo. -

- This hole is cursed, we had to have scheduled the work for the hole in the floor - Lázaro replied.

- The plant hole is smoking. - Yoel told him - A week ago they chased the Chinese over there and they almost caught him, but don't despair and wait, click the matchbox again.

Lázaro listened to his friend with the same result and told him: -Brother, in this circumstance we have no choice but to make a decision, because what we bring does not accept return. Read the label so you realize we can't return it to where we picked it up.

Silvio interrupted them, visibly upset: - And then guys, what can we do now? Did we bring it from so far to now come here to lose it? It is very sad.

- Stick to the nose of the canal entrance - Lázaro said, taking control of the situation - I'm going to disembark and reconnoiter the area to see what happens, because we can't keep wasting time. It's going to take us 12 noon in this situation. I'm going to check the hole and if I don't give you a signal with the matchbox in 10 minutes, take this out of here and hide it in the mangrove. I think that the most convenient thing is that they hide it in the hollow of the chapín that is near here and that you know very well. That hole is very cold because we haven't worked on it for a long time, but be very careful because the tide breaks and you can run aground. Remember that this team comes well loaded, nail everything well hidden and tomorrow it will dawn and we will see, because if the monkey is in the hole waiting, the safest thing is that I will be arrested on suspicion. But now let's not waste any more time, stick to the entrance nose.

This mental process of weighing the long-term consequences of each trip was routine in the lives of Lázaro, Yoel, and many other smugglers in the area. It's called "living on the edge, dangerously" and it was what many of them liked best about this job. Perhaps to any other mortal they sound like excuses for lawless people, willing to commit crimes for the love of money. It is logical to think that, but it is certainly difficult to understand their consciences without having lived through those moments. That's why the smartest thing, in my opinion, is to give them the benefit of the doubt.

Yoel didn't wait long and stuck the prow of the boat to the promontory that was at the end of the channel and Lázaro jumped to land like a cat.

Yoel exclaimed when he saw him jump like a monkey: -I think this one is faster than me, and that he is older..

Lázaro was lost in the dark. The Arrow took off the launch again from the end of the channel and they began to wait for the signal from Lázaro. After several endless minutes they saw three flashes in the distance. It was the matchbox. Silvio, unable to contain his emotion, said to his companions:

- The signal, let's go inside. -

Yoel steered the boat down the narrow canal toward the rough wooden cabinet and slammed it against it.

Silvio jumped to meet Lázaro, and Lázaro told him: - Go to the entrance of the canal and watch out for someone who is not invited to the birthday party.

Lázaro had made this decision for two reasons: first, so as not to be surprised during the unloading operation, and second, to distance Silvio from knowing where he would nail the 56 packages, because of the entire group, he was the least reliable and more dangerous.

Then he turned to Jairo and told him: -Go into the cabin and start taking out the packages. give them to me - The 56 40-pound packages felt like 100 100-pound ones. One by one they emerged from the boat's galley. They had to be hidden in the woods in total darkness, a darkness where not a single hand could be seen. This maneuver had been done too many times in the past, it no longer had a mystery. But if the danger of being discovered by thieves or the authorities. Either way they would be lost. Hiding them now, at least they had a chance to return to look for them at another time, during the day, without the danger that the night represents.

Jairo, with a package on his shoulder, commented: - Easy money, right, the one who doesn't know is like the one he doesn't see. -

Jairo took the packages out of the cabin and Lázaro hid it in the bush, and in an hour between the 3 while Silvio watched the road. They had made a huge effort but in the end all the drug packages were hidden in the mangrove.

Then they all boarded the boat, and although they were very tired, they left for the lighthouse and from there to the open sea to clean the boat well. They could not leave even the smallest seed, because any evidence of what they had brought, they risked losing the boat. Although the worst was over, there was still the possibility of having an encounter with some authority boat on the way to Miami. And if they checked their pot, taking into account the racial profile of all of them, and they found a single seed, they would all go to jail.

Many times the police themselves planted the evidence. They carried the seed in their mouths and spit it out into the boat maliciously. In short, if they were unlucky enough to run into any patrol, they would miss the boat and be arrested for complying with the minimum tolerance law, in force in those days when marijuana was something worse than alcohol, tobacco and weapons. of fire.

"Now we have to clean the party room well," Lázaro said, adding irony to the word party.

Yoel added: - This work is hard, but we have to do it. -

Once moored to the dock at Crandon Park, the exhausted crew, aided by detergent and brooms, busied themselves with whitewashing the crime scene. They swept the boat throwing sea water that the boat's bilge pumps took care of removing.

Lázaro washed a white T-shirt that had turned green. The sea turned rough, the wind kicked up the waves, and they hurried to finish the cleanup. At the end of the disinfection they headed north. It was already dawn and everyone was very tired, but happy because the first stage of the work had been completed.

They arrived at the house of Yoel el Flecha and Lázaro told him:

- I'm going to call Manolo to find out why he didn't come to wait for us, and I'm going to tell him to get ready for tonight and help us pick up the merchandise in the mooring hole, not even Jairo can get in touch with his bosses , the Murillo family, or Silvio with his people.
They all agreed to go to an apartment owned by Yoel the Arrow on SW 104th Street and 107th Avenue, across from Miami Dade College. A bachelor apartment where everyone got comfortable as they could and fell asleep overcome by sleep.

At around 4pm, he was woken up by the ringing of the doorbell, Yoel jumped awake and opened the door. It was Manolo who came to look for them, but very well accompanied, to pick up what they had left hidden in the mangrove in the hole where the moored.

- How is everything horse? How did it go? - was Manolo's greeting.

Yoel replied: - Everything is fine brother, if it gets better it breaks; we are ready for the fight.

Manolo told him that the Murillo brothers' sailboat had had a problem on the island of San Andrés, that it would not arrive on time, and he recommended that they not go to the hole so as not to heat it up.

Lázaro entered the kitchen while Flecha was brewing coffee and told Manolo angrily: - From now on, when we're out, you're going to wait for us and you're only going to suspend the trip on a direct order from Yoel or mine, a loud command.

At that moment Silvio and Jairo entered the kitchen, Lázaro addressed them and told them: - Everything is ready, the refrigerated truck is outside to move the fish -

Indeed, Manolo and Rosendo had a refrigerated truck, like the one commonly used to bring shellfish from the Florida Keys to Miami fishmongers. The truck was a perfect alibi to avoid suspicion.

- It's very good, but now please go to the Chinese restaurant on 137th and 88th and buy a familiar fried rice, or better two specials with all the irons and two Chinese soups also familiar and four portions of chicken wings with honey for Eat before leaving, asked Lázaro.

The rest of the group took a shower and then had no choice but to put on the wet clothes they had brought from the day before. Wet and dirty, smelling of marijuana, because Yoel the Arrow is too skinny and his clothes don't fit anyone.

After eating fried rice, Chinese soup and chicken wings in honey and of course Cuban coffee brewed by Lázaro, they left for the moored hole. Manolo and Yoel boarded the truck of the fishmonger named Garcia and sons. Silvio, Jairo, Rosendo and Lázaro followed them in a red Ford Bronco owned by Lázaro.

They took the Florida Turnpike heading south and reached Florida City and, as was customary they stopped at the

Shark Fish Market, where they bought everything they needed to form the spectacle of joyful fishermen. They bought bait, ice, chips and soft drinks. They didn't need anything else because Lázaro had everything else in his truck, all the necessary fishing gear in case the flies, or rather, if they collided with any patrol of the authority, Florida Marine Patrol, customs and conservation of animal life.

They left the shark to take an old road and went over the camel bridge that divides Monroe and Dade counties. Lázaro had been a little late to let the fishmonger's truck enter the moored hole first. The refrigerated truck entered the narrow path between the mangroves. Then the Bronco entered, and Lázaro left Jairo at the entrance to the hole with a radius of 2 meters so that he could serve as a lookout and give the alarm of the visit of an intruder. When Lázaro, Rosendo and Silvio reached the end of the road that connects with the sea, Yoel el Flecha and Manolo were already finishing the job of loading the last package.

Lázaro called Jairo on the radio and asked him: - Boy, tell me, how are things at your house? Is Tarzan over there? - Lázaro was referring to the Tarzan who is always accompanied by the monkey Chita, and the monkey is the name given to the Police in the popular Cuban heat.

"I don't see the king of the jungle around here," answered Jairo.

- Silvio you go in the fishmonger's truck with Yoel and leave 12 packages, which are our payment, at Rosendo's farm. Lázaro said.

Silvio protested: - Lázaro is not 12, it is 11. -

- There are 12, because if it hadn't been for us, you would have lost everything -Yoel the Arrow told him.

Silvio understood, at that moment, that it was useless to argue, Lázaro was right and had good reasons to claim that extra package.

When Lázaro referred to Rosendo's farm, he did so referring to a small 5-acre farm that Rosendo had on 184th Street in Southwest Miami, in what is known as Reed Land.

-Okay brother, I'll take Silvio with me and then I'll help you deliver the merchandise to his owners, count on me in everything I can collaborate-

When he said goodbye, Silvio gave Lázaro a big hug and told him: - You've thrown me a tremendous towel, and I'll always keep that in mind. -

Yoel and Silvio left in the fishmonger's truck, reached the entrance to the hole in the old road and headed south towards Cayo Largo so as not to have to cross the camel bridge, where the toll that divides the counties is. Lázaro knew that the employees who collected the ticket had a police complex and served as an informer for the real police. They reached the junction with US1 and headed north from there; Lázaro, Rosendo, Manolo and Jairo followed him at a safe distance in the Ford Bronco.

Silvio turned to Yoel and told him: - Roll down the window and put on some music that scares the monkey.

- Leave the superstitions that what is for you, nobody takes it away from you, and when it's your turn, even if you take it off and when it's not your turn, even if you wear it.

"Partner, it's not superstition, it's popular psychology," Silvio replied with a smile on his lips, the kind that comes when someone realizes that he could already breathe easy, that the worst was behind him.

Yoel thought that Silvio might be right. He rolled down the window and turned the radio on a Latin station where a song by Frankie Ruiz, a famous Puerto Rican singer who was Lázaro's cellmate, was playing:

> *"And how they do it - I don't know*
> *What is the business - do you know..."*

They raced north on US-1 and reached the most dangerous part of the road, Florida City. The truck turned onto 177th Avenue and the Bronco turned onto the Florida Turnpike. They had divided so as not to make a caravan. Yoel and Silvio with the fishmonger's truck went up to 184th street of SW Eureka and there they turned right to reach Rosendo's farm, where they left the 12 packages that were the boatmen's payment. After leaving the 12 packages Yoel and Silvio went to deliver the packages to the owners of the work

Finishing everything, Yoel the Arrow called Lázaro by phone and told him: - Pigeon in a cage, Paloma flew, mission accomplished, see you tomorrow because today I'm too tired. Call Ernesto to offer him what we have and pay attention to the price, no less than 500 varos per pound. -

"Okay," Lázaro replied.

- See you tomorrow at the office - Yoel said before hanging up.

They called "the office" the El Floridita bar on 22nd Avenue and NW Third Street, where they occasionally met. There they dispatched their businesses drinking Yoel beer and Lázaro mineral water. There the two friends talked with the titis, the Central American employees of the bar who, in exchange for a good tip, gave them protection.

The next day, around noon, Yoel and Lázaro met at the bar, and together they went to have fish for lunch. They picked Garcia's shrimp farm, the fish market on Flagler Street and SW 18th Avenue; next to the El Libanés supermarket.

While they were enjoying a very good fish soup and eating a fry, waiting for 2 snapper filets that were being fried, Yoel explained to Lázaro: - The crazy man already picked up the material I gave him, he told me he would pay 500 dollars for pound and that in the evening he would give me the money.

"It would have been a very good deal if Silvio had left us the rest of the merchandise to sell it and we would have found something else at the sale," Lázaro said to his friend.

"I asked him, but he says that in New York he could get more money from him," answered Yoel.

- Is Miguel going to take that merchandise so far, driving all the way alone? Lázaro asked.

- He was not alone, he was accompanied by two individuals, supposedly his partners and friends, I think they were the owners of the job because they are both Colombians and because of their accent I think they were coastal people from Barranquilla or samariums - answered Yoel, el Flecha.

- And do you know any of them? Lázaro asked.

-No, I have never seen them in my life, I only know because I heard Silvio pronounce his names, that one is called Salim and the other Pacho. The third was called Alfonso.

"But those were the ones who had problems with him," Lázaro said to his friend. "Supposedly they were looking for him to kill him."

- I don't know what you're talking about, Julito, from what I could see and appreciate, he had a lot of trust and friendship. Yoel replied.

- What happens is that you are not aware of the story. - Lázaro said - Do you remember the problem that Silvio had years ago? What cost the lives of Aracel, el Gordo and Julito, el Paisa? Well, those are the guys who set the trap for them to justify a large amount of money that some Colombian drug lords supposedly owed him. They had to deliver some heads and it fell to those unhappy boys to pay the maximum price.

- The one who is not aware of anything is you, my partner. - Yoel replied - What happened was that Silvio realized that Henry wanted to hand him over to blame him for the robbery,
he called his boss in Cuba, Major Camejo, from a public telephone on the road back and told him what was happening. This, after consulting with his superiors, called the Murillo brothers, with whom they had worked for a long time, to help Silvio get out of this problem alive. Henry couldn't find out, because he would immediately lose confidence in the Colombians and, worst of all, he would believe that the debt had not yet been paid. The plan was for Silvio to say that he had the money hidden and one of Henry's men, who actually worked for the Murillo's, to go with him to look for it. The deal was that Silvio would keep $300,000 of the half million and they would then help him hide in California with the rest of the money, until the matter cooled down. -

- What a liar this shithead is. - Lazaro said, unable to believe what he was hearing.

-Wait, this doesn't end there, -said Yoel- what he told you about the police station is a lie, the only truth is that he left his friends at the mercy of those criminals to save his skin. In the end, as you know very well, Henry and his henchmen beat Aracel and Julito to death after torturing them, while Silvio calmly left with his money for California. Tremendous friend that he was. -

- Ñoooooooo, how heavy, bro! So this guy practically had his friends killed. - Lazaro reacted with disgust.

- Yes of course! You well know that all of us who are in this business do not have the same honor or the same principles, they are not all family, most are occasional accomplices. But these were his childhood friends, all Marielitos, who had known each other all their lives. When I heard that story I felt sick to my stomach. -Yoel said with sadness in his eyes, which mixed with the fatigue and nerves of the last few hours made him look like an old man.

-If what you say is the truth, -said Lázaro visibly concerned- from now on with Silvio you have to be very careful, he told me a very different story, he lied to me blatantly. He made me believe that he was saved by a miracle, entering a police station and that he had tricked the hit man. But according to what you tell me, everything was fixed and they released him without any problem. -

Yes, and that same gunman who was supposed to kill him, he collected the money and took it to the Murillo's. That was all fixed. - Yoel commented, seeing Lazaro's surprised face.

- You have left me with my mouth open, my son, and I believed every word! -

"It was like that," replied Yoel. -I thought you knew his story and that you were fine with that. When I saw Silvio appear in the marina and you received him with a smile, although he seemed a bit strange to me, he gave me the impression

that he you had forgiven what he did. Or at least it didn't
bother you. -

- Forgive? Never! Friends are sacred, but when you grew
up with them, you experienced the same shit that we all
experienced in Cuba. They lived together! I will never
forgive him for what he did, and when I see him again I will
ask him to tell me the truth and explain to me how he was
capable of such a betrayal. - Lazaro said, visibly angry.

He paused because the waitress had arrived with the fried
snappers and put them on the table. The woman quietly
withdrew because she realized that the guests were talking
about something very serious.

- Although I doubt very much that I want to see him again. -
added Lazaro, already a little calmer after the interruption -
I know that many of us are criminals, but even among us
there is a code of honor. Family and friends are respected,
cared for. Whoever lets his friends die like this, to blows,
deserves a special place in hell.

Lazaro looked down and started eating his fried snapper,
he didn't want it to get cold.

CHAPTER 4

OPERATION ALI BABA

- Yesterday black Arthur called me, and he wants us to see him in Bimini as soon as possible, he told me he has a job for us - Lázaro said to his friend while looking at the menu, sitting at the table of the restaurant / office where they passed most of the time they remained on dry land.

- And what do you want to do? - Yoel asked him.

- We can go to Manolo, you and I in the Corza, I'm going to call him to wait for us at the Hotel Amarillo on Saturday. -

As planned on Saturday morning, the three friends left Miami heading east. At noon it was already entering the canal and 10 minutes later the boat was moored at the Bron dock. It was mandatory to go through the customs office to regularize their stay on the island, so after doing the paperwork and giving the official the mandatory $100 "tip" that bought silence, they went straight to Mama's inn to have lunch. Upon entering the door they found 4 Cubans sitting at a table who, upon seeing them, acted nervously, as if they were waiting for them.

Manolo, surprised at not knowing any of them, spoke first:

- Do you come from Miami? -

- No, we come from Panama, - one of them replied.

- Do you come from Panama by boat? - Manolo asked him again.

- No, we came from Panama by plane - replied Rosendo, which was the name of that Cuban.

In the late 1980s, a secret agreement was signed between the government of the Republic of Panama, under the presidency of General Antonio Manuel Noriega, and the Cuban Ministry of the Interior to create what looks very much like a modern slave sales. Noriega sold visas to the Cuban Ministry of the Interior at a rate of 4,000 dollars per person, and those who wanted to leave the island could buy them for $9,000 from the Castro government through the MC, a division of the MININT created especially to generate profits for the revolution and circumvent the North American blockade. The director of the MC was, until his death, Colonel Antonio de la Guardia, one of those shot by the Castro government in 1989.

Four thousand dollars for Noriega and 5 thousand for the Cuban MC: a great deal. But those who could leave Cuba had to go to Panama and find a way to reach their final destination, which for many was the United States of America.

The journey from Central America and the southern border was, and still is, extremely dangerous. So a Cuban from Miami, owner of a two-engine D18 plane, came up with the brilliant idea of generating profit with the desperation of the people and began to fly Cubans from Panama to the Bahamas Islands.

As the Cubans give everything a name, they began to call it "La Palangana" because the plane was in terrible condition, and those who traveled on it were called "los palangana".

Palanganeros were the 4 Cubans who were sitting at that table in Mama's fonda.

Lázaro called the owner and told her:

- Put in my account what my countrymen consume. -Later he turned to Rosendo and asked him: -Are you the only Cubans on the Island?

- No member, the Hotel Amarillo is full - answered Rosendo, the Cuban who spoke the most in the group. The others seemed tired, shy or scared.

- Who comes in front of you? Yoel asked him.

- No one comes to the front, everyone travels on their own.

- And how do you plan to get to Florida? Lázaro asked again.

- Well brother, that is in the hands of my family in Miami and in the hands of God.

- And your family in Miami has a boat? Manuel asked.

- I don't know, but they will know what they have to do. Keeping us here will be more expensive than in Cuba.

The four Cubans finished lunch, thanked Lázaro, and walked to the Amarillo Hotel.

Manolo commented:

- Communism has made our countrymen in Cuba lose the financial responsibility they have after being of legal age. In Cuba it is believed that the people of Miami always have to maintain them. And they shout loudly "the Americans have to give us".

They all nodded. After eating and paying the bill, they went to the Amarillo Hotel to rent a room and wait for Arthur there.

They arrived at the hotel, settled into their rooms and then went upstairs to talk to the Cubans who had arrived in the basin. Lázaro, seeing the conditions in which they were living and also out of compassion and respect for his compatriots, distributed 2,000 dollars among the Cubans. basins. He left everyone saying thank you and then went down to the marina to fill the boat's gas tank. Yoel and Manolo stayed talking with the panganeros.

First Manolo came down and Lázaro asked him:

- And Yoel, why didn't he come down too?

"He was talking to a Cuban lady who comes with her daughters," answered Manolo.

- And how old are the lady and the daughters? Lázaro asked.

- I think the mother is 45 or 50 years old and the girls are 18 or 20 years old, because there are two of them.

- And how do they look? - Lázaro asked again.

- The old woman is a peasant who looks average, but the girls are two pieces of candy.

They were in that conversation when they saw Yoel arrive, and Lázaro, addressing him, said:

- Don't even think about it, we came to talk to Arthur and nothing else.

- Are you a fortune teller now? Yoel asked him.

- I'm not a fortune teller, but I know you - Lázaro replied.

- And what do you think? Yoel asked Manolo.

- Don't get me in trouble, I'm just the mechanic, but the Bible says: Do good and don't look at who -

- Well, one philanthropist and the other evangelical, we are going to wait for Arthur to arrive and then decide - Lázaro finished with a half smile on his face. He knew that he had half the battle lost. -

They didn't have to wait long, because that same night Arthur arrived. But he was alone, he arrived accompanied by a man he introduced as a Panamanian named Noel Camejo.

- Nice to meet you, I'm Lazaro, this is Yoel and this is Manolo. - Surnames never, it was a custom among smugglers to give the least amount of personal information.

The 5 of them went to the hotel room, once inside Arthur spoke:

- This man is Camejo, he has merchandise in Sabana del Mar, Jamaica, and a ship in the Florida Keys. He only needs two good sailors to go to Jamaica and bring her to Florida.

- And what are we talking about? Lázaro asked.

- 5 thousand pounds of seedless yerba mate - Camejo replied.

- And what kind of boat? - was Yoel's question.

- A 50-foot long Grand Bank, with two double-turbo 3208 Caterpillar engines and a thousand gallons of oil in a tank - Camejo replied.

- And with a thousand gallons? I don't think it's enough to go back and forth - Yoel asked them.

- At that point is where we are going to have the least problems, because we can navigate in Cuban waters and in Cabo de San Antonio they can give us oil - replied Camejo.

- And who is going to authorize us to do that? Lázaro asked.

- The MC Department of the Ministry of the Interior and the Cuban Navy - replied Camejo with a knowing smile.

- To be able to do business of this kind, the first thing we have to do is not lie, - Lazaro said very seriously - you say you're from Panama, but I don't think so, you're Cuban, and if you're from Panama, He is from a neighborhood that is called that and is in Marianao.

- Yes, Lázaro is right, I am Cuban, and I am an officer of the Cuban Navy, that is why I speak to you with such certainty - Camejo replied.

- From what you say, are the Cuban Navy and the Ministry of the Interior going to protect us? Lázaro asked.

- And what proof do we have of that? Yoel asked.

- First my word, and second something that I am going to explain to you, the MC of the Ministry of the Interior is a Department created to break the blockade and collect foreign exchange, the merchandise that we are going to take where it can best be sold is in the United States and with With that money we will be able to buy things that Cuba needs. Without your help we cannot do anything, if the operation fails, the ones who are going to lose the most are us - explained Camejo.

- If the trip falls through, Cuba loses what it paid for the merchandise and what it cost to buy the ship, more or less half a million dollars, which for anyone is a lot of money - Yoel told them, and added - : It's your plan. and you're leaving with us, aren't you?

- When do we go? Camejo asked.

- And do you have papers Mr. Camejo? Lázaro asked.

- Yes, I have Panamanian papers with a US visa.

- Well, what we came for, Manolo and Yoel can go pouring gasoline while I paint the Hotel and fire Arthur - Lázaro ordered.

Lázaro arrived next to the boat and found everything ready to leave, but not with 4 passengers, but with seven, because between Yoel and Manolo they had agreed and they had the three basins sitting on the seat, next to the engines, the lady and her daughters. Lázaro didn't say a word because, in his mind, he had already approved the favor and didn't want to insult anyone. He thought of his family, his friends and all the people he himself helped to leave Cuba and remembered that those actions soften the soul and create good karma.

Between Camejo and Manolo they loosened ropes, and with Yoel at the helm the boat began to leave through the channel.

The Ali Baba operation had begun.

- Don't worry brother, women are cold - Yoel said in a low voice to Lázaro.

- Yes, of course they get cold, but if they catch us with 3 illegals we lose the boat and even Camejo goes to jail, but really we have to do good - Lázaro replied.

As someone who does good and above all without interest, has earned a place in heaven, everything went well that day and Manolo and Yoel accompanied Teresa, Caridad and Barbarita, which was the name of the three Cubans, to Little Havana to the house of one of Teresa's brothers, where they were invited to have coffee for any reward.

Lázaro, meanwhile, took Camejo to Cayo Maratón where the Ali Baba was moored, which was the name of the Grand Bank boat that would take them on another new adventure together with their former enemies transformed into allies and where the Cuban officer would spend the night.

"Money has that strange quality of bringing people together," Lazaro thought as he drove, recalling that for most of his adult life he had felt a deep hatred of the Cuban regime. Three bullet holes in his body did not let him forget.

The next day the three partners met in the apartment of the beautiful Sofía, Lázaro's favorite friend, and after lunch and coffee, Lázaro spoke:

- Gentlemen, this is a very delicate matter and we must do it in the greatest reserve, strictly confidential.

- And do you think we can trust this Camejo, who according to him is a man from the apparatus? - Manolo told them.

- This is a gambling game in everything, if we lose, he loses too, because the merchandise is worth nothing until it reaches the yuma, where the money is, that of the Jamaicans, that of the Cubans and ours.

- We have to decide now, I'm willing to do the job. He who risks nothing wins nothing, and we have always taken risks. - Lazaro commented looking straight into Yoel's eyes.

- Well, if you believe that, let go of the deer - Yoel told him.

- I'm not going to stay on land, I'm going with you - Manolo told them.

Lázaro took the phone and called the number that Camejo had given him, spoke with him and addressed his companions:

-Camejo is waiting for us at a farm in Homestead, he gave me the address. The farm is called El Cantero.

- Well, go ahead and let's knock it down - Manolo told them.

At the farm they met Camejo, and the meeting was joined by Luis el Grande and El Moto, the other members of Lazaro's group, and after the formalities Luis took the floor and without wasting time asked them:

- What plans do you have to do this work? Camejo has already explained to me what it is about. -

Lázaro, the one with the most experience in the matter, took the floor:

- According to what Mr. Camejo explained to us, our job is to bring something from Jamaica that you have there in Sabana del Mar and for this purpose you are going to provide us with a Grand Bank with a thousand gallons of oil.

The Moto interrupted Lázaro:

- A new package ship that makes 20 mutes.

Lázaro continued:

- Camejo also explained to us how much sailing to Jamaica, that coming from it we could navigate in Cuban waters, and that if there was any problem with the oil, the Cubans could hit us at Cape San Antonio.

- That is so - confirmed Luis.

- If things are like this, it can be deduced that we are working with the Cuban Government.

Lázaro was interrupted by Camejo.

- Not with the Cuban government, we are working with MC.

- And what is actually MC? Yoel asked.

- MC is a department - Camejo replied.

- A department of what ministry in Cuba? Yoel asked again.

- From the Ministry of the Interior - replied Camejo.

Again, without taking his finger off the line, Yoel told him:

- From the Ministry of the Interior of the Cuban government, I understand that this is working with the Cuban government, yes you can navigate within its waters, yes they can give us oil in case of need, because with the control that you have nobody can do anything well, if it is not authorized well from above.

Again Yoel was interrupted by Camejo.

- That authorized good from above, is relative.

- Relating to what? - asked him this time Lázaro.

Camejo didn't have to think long to answer.

- Regarding everything going well, you should know that victory has many fathers, but defeat is an orphan.

Yoel took up the word again.

- As you are going to accompany us in case of need, the ideal thing would be for you to get along with your people. But we haven't talked about something very important yet, which is how much we're going to earn, or the details of the job.

- You will have a quarter of the net profit, and you must make a plan - Camejo replied.

Lázaro hastened to speak:

- As I understand that you do not think of sticking to Florida with such a slow and loaded boat, my plan is to take the merchandise in the Ali Baba to Anguilla in the Bank of Cayo Sal and from there by speedboat to Marathon, boats that , of course they will be from us.

Lazaro paused and stared at the Cuban soldier:

- With all due respect, Mr. Camejo, I believe that they take us somewhat hard in the payment. -

Always negotiating the price was a daily habit among drug traffickers, never giving the appearance that the payment was sufficient, thus keeping the commissions high. In most cases the strategy worked and in this case, in the case of the Cuban government, a good work dynamic could be generated or in the long term, with millions in profit.

- It is special merchandise, first-class merchandise, without seed, and you are going to be able to sell it, I think you can earn more from the sale than from the trip - El Moto told them, who until now had barely opened his mouth and asked: - How is the plan? Who is going in the Ali Baba, who is going to wait at the Bank of Cayo Sal, and who is going to be on land to bring the merchandise here? -

Silence fell. Lázaro meditated for a moment and finally explained:

- According to my plan, Camejo, Moto, Yoel and I can go to Ali Baba. On the island of Anguilla they will wait for us at La Corza with Manolo and El Moto and on land Luis el Grande can wait for us.

- I see that plan very well - replied Camejo.

- Me too - Luis told them.

Luis was a retired CIA agent who, instead of spending his old age picking tomatoes in Homestead, decided to turn to rattling to ensure a good old age.

The Moto nodded positively and four days later the Ali Baba sailed through the Caribbean Sea bound for Jamaica, manned by Major Camejo of the Cuban Navy.

- Put 120 degrees on the compass, we are going to pass through the south of Isla de Pino - Lázaro ordered Yoel.

- Isle of Youth - I try to correct Camejo.

"Isla de la Juventud for you, Mayor Camejo, for my Isla de Pino," Lázaro replied.

Camejo understood and did not answer him for the second time.

At dusk they sailed south of Cayo Largo, then below the Jardines de la Reina Archipelago and in an hour they reached the coast of Jamaica. There they loaded 170 packages of 30 pounds per package, a total of 5,100 pounds of seedless marijuana, which at the market price at that time, which was approximately 600 dollars per pound, made a total of 3,600,000 dollars.

As agreed, $765,000 would go to Lazaro's group and the rest $2,295,000 would go to the Cuban Ministry of the Interior.

Leaving Jamaica, Lázaro ordered the Moto at the helm:

- To the northeast we will navigate between the keys of the Jardines de la Reina and Cuba. Now we are going to know to what extent the MC has power because the Ministry of the Interior is one thing and the Cuban Navy is another thing.

- Yes, partner, now we are going to see to what extent this smuggling operation has the green light from the Cuban government - Yoel told him.

- And I've told you that everything is authorized at the highest level, as long as everything goes well - Camejo replied.

This comment from the Cuban elder made something very clear that Lazaro always suspected: as long as they don't discover the crime, everything is fine. But if for some reason the US government intercepts the drug shipment, official Cuban policy was to deny any knowledge of the smuggling and to accuse those involved as if they were acting in their own interests. Such hypocrisy was always reflected in Cuba's official position regarding drug trafficking. After the trials of Ochoa, De la Guardia and

Abrahantes, Fidel Castro announced that the problem of drug trafficking in Cuba had ended. However, it was evident that what the Cuban dictator was trying to do was get rid of international pressure and avoid a North American invasion at all costs, as happened to Noriega in 1989.

The group sailed to the south of the province of Camagüey with a calm sea and it was there that Major Camejo gave proof of where the authorization he had came from.

Calling the Cabo de San Antonio Border Unit, after speaking on the shortwave radio, he addressed his fellow travelers:

- In front of Cabo de San Antonio, in international waters, the gringo coast guard is anchored, the Dallas, the one that releases the balloon with the radar; I don't think it's prudent to go on and get into the lion's den.

- And what do you advise to do? Lázaro asked.

- We have two options, enter Cienfuegos or Cayo Largo del Sur and wait there for the gringo coastguard to move, because continuing is very dangerous. And even if we stick to the island, he's going to follow us, and when we go out into the gulf he's going to hunt us down and split us in two. So you choose: either Cienfuegos or Cayo Largo.

"Key Largo," Yoel told him.

- Cayo Largo - Lázaro and Manolo said in chorus.

- I'm going to call by radio so that they wait for us in Cayo Largo del Sur and I'm going to reserve 4 rooms at the Pelicano Hotel - Major Camejo told them.

- And why so many rooms? Yoel asked.

- It will dawn and you will see - replied Camejo with a smile.

- What is Mayor smiling about? Lázaro asked.

- They'll see, they'll see - answered Camejo.

A few hours later the Ali Baba moored her lines in Cayo Largo del Sur, a paradise in the Caribbean reserved at that time only for foreign tourists. They arrived and after each one occupied his room they went to dinner. The Cuban people did not even see that type of food in a movie: pasta with lobster, beef steak with vegetables, a seafood soup and others dishes that would make any neighbor in the area envious.

Already having coffee, Major Camejo, a member of the most hypocritical party in the world, the Cuban Communist Party, asked his fellow adventurers:

- I'm going to call Cuba so that my girlfriend can come with me. Do you prefer me to come alone, or bring some friends?

- No, Camejo, don't bring a company, bring a battalion - answered Yoel smiling, excited.

- And company of whom and for what? - Lázaro asked, who played the goat with nonsense from time to time.

- Don't worry brother, if you don't want company I'll keep yours - Moto told him.

- They had already told me about that and I didn't believe it, tell me what you presume and I'll tell you what you lack, live to see - Lázaro told him, who was the romantic of the group. On that occasion he came to understand that there are things that, even if they are not in your way of feeling, cannot be avoided, because man is an animal with reason, but desire exceeds sanity.

- And when do the reinforcements arrive? - Yoel asked Camejo.

- Tomorrow on the plane at 10 in the morning, we have to go to the airport for them, - replied the Major, who had become not only a smuggler, but also a pimp.

A long night for those waiting for the Three Wise Men, who this time were not Melchor, Gaspar and Baltasar, but Laura, Maciel, Ady and Lorena. Four dolls barely defending themselves in a country in complete material and moral ruin.

That morning, while they waited for the little Russian Antonov with two engines to make the trip from the José Martí airport in Rancho Boyero in Havana to Cayo Largo del Sur, Lázaro, Yoel and Manolo went for a walk on the beach.

Lázaro began the talk with a question:

- How do you understand that Mayor Camejo's girlfriend comes to visit him? As far as I know, he is a married man with children.

Yoel looked at Lázaro with a smile and said:

- Don't play the new Lázaro, you don't know that in Cuba there is an escort service that the people call prostitutes, that to live a little better they accompany foreigners.

- But they accompany where? Lázaro asked.

- To bed partner, to bed, to walk, to dance, everywhere - answered Manolo and the three of them started laughing.

- It is incredible that these people, who boasted of morals, now promote the oldest profession of humanity. Before, the woman used to do it because she liked it, now they do it so as not to go hungry, said Manolo.

- They're not all like that either. There are some who do it because they like it - answered Yoel.

Lázaro ended by saying:

-The decent woman lends it, the lover gives it, the one who doesn't understand love, she sells it. From this it follows that whoever does not lend it, gives it or sells it.

It was evident that Lázaro was the romantic of the group, who sometimes played dumb to provoke thoughts in others.

- All of this is true, but if the girls come with the supposed girlfriend of Major Camejo, who is a man from the apparatus, a man who is actually our political enemy, and who is here today for the same thing as us, for money, we have to be very careful what we say in front of them - Yoel warned.

- The coast guard thing in the Cape could be a hoax to bring us here and blackmail us, they are specialists in doing that - said Lázaro.

- Everything is very nice, but a lot of kindness confuses me - ended up saying Yoel.

From the beach they returned to the hotel. They had declined the trip to the airport so as not to show a mask, in someone else's yard. Upon arriving at the hotel, the Navy Major and MC agent, Camejo, was already waiting for them with the girls, who seemed chosen for a beauty contest. Since the woman is the only animal that chooses the hunter, they waited for the girls to make their selection. Teresa took Camejo by the hand, Maciel took El Moto, Lorena took Yoel, Adela took Manolo and Laura took Lázaro. Later they found out, through the girls, that these selections had not actually been made by them but by Camejo, according to the profile he had made of each one of them.

- The girls left Havana early and must be hungry. Let's all go to lunch - suggested Camejo.

That suggestion was approved unanimously. In Cuba almost always everything is approved unanimously. The 4 couples went to the hotel restaurant.

The whole group, without measure in formalities, ate lavishly. Afterwards, each one goes to her room to do something that does not need to be described in this book because it is older than humanity itself. Moreover, it is the reason why the human race exists.

After a week living in paradise, Camejo arrived with the good/bad news that the gringo coastguard had sailed northwest and that they could continue their march. The men headed for the sea and the girls headed for the Antonov, heading for Cuba. Before separating, Lázaro, Yoel and Manolo promised to help them get to the United States, which was actually what they all wanted to achieve.

The Ali Baba, already loaded, sailed the entire north coast of Cuba up to Varadero, from where they sailed towards the bank of Cayo Sal to the islet of Anguila. They stayed to the east of the islet to the heave, because it was very dangerous to drop anchor there.

- I knew that with this bad weather Manolo would not be able to arrive on time - commented Yoel.

- And why didn't they leave earlier? Camejo asked him.

- In this place you can't make time, here you have to arrive, load, and fly away. Over this bank fly the plane of the blacks and the plane of the American Coast Guard. This here is pure gunpowder - Lázaro explained.

- We have to implement plan B - Yoel told them.

- And what is plan B? - Moto asked him.

- We are going to stick the boat as far as possible to the island, we are going to lower the packages and hide them in the mangrove, and then we take off a little and start fishing and when Manolo arrives, we load the boat - explained Yoel, that he had already had to do that before.

- But quickly, here with that upstairs we are on fire - Lázaro told him.

With the speed that a deer runs after a tiger, the 4 men took the boat to the sand of the beach and in an hour they had the packages hidden inside the mangrove of the island. They then sailed about 5 miles to the center of the bank and started fishing.

Half an hour later the United States Coast Guard reconnaissance plane was flying low over them.

- In less than an hour they will be here - Lázaro told them.

- Who's going to be here? - asked Major Camejo, thinking of Manolo.

- The Americans can't enter the bank - Moto said.

- But blacks do - answered Yoel who had spoken with the knowledge that experience gives.

And he was quite right, because it didn't take long for the small plane of the Bahamas Island Defense Forces to fly over them.

"Let's move to the docks," Yoel told him.

- No, Yoel. Head towards Los Perros, we are closer to the Canal de San Nicolás there.

They could not reach the Perros, which are a group of stones in the northeast of the bank of Cayo Sal, because they were stopped by the Great Inagua frigate of the Bahamas.

- If someone brings a weapon, throw it into the water, and if someone catches something, throw the fish into the water. We cannot give you the slightest reason to take us to Nassau - Lázaro told him.

- I had to stay on the island in case Manolo arrives - Yoel said.

- We are going to put Plan C into action, after the blacks leave for Marathon, we have to wait for it to get very cold to be able to get the merchandise out of the island. If we are not very intelligent we can lose everything - Lázaro told him.

- But how is the sea, not even Manolo could jump the channel, and we are not going to be able to do it either - Camejo told them.

- Major, Manolo comes in a 30-foot boat, and we are sailing in a 50-foot horse with two 3208 engines. It may be hard for us, but we crossed, we crossed, with strong seas, and little engine - he finished Yoel saying.

Yoel was absolutely right because 6 hours later, they passed by the Faro del Sombrero on their way to the pier where La Corza is moored.

- What are you doing here? Manolo asked him.

"It's a long story," Yoel replied.

- As soon as the wind falls, Yoel, you and I are going to look for what we left in Anguilla - Lázaro told him.

- And are we going to put it here? Manolo asked him.

- No, not here, we're going to tie up - Lázaro replied.

As expected, the wind slackened and the Corza manned by Manolo, Yoel and Lázaro went out to finish the Ali Baba operation, a joint operation of the MC and the Navy of the Republic of Cuba with the collaboration of Cuban boatmen, which According to what Major Camejo had said, it was authorized to the highest level of command in Cuba.

Already sailing towards the Bank of Cayo Sal with Yoel at the helm of the boat, Lázaro at his side, and Manolo sitting on the seat next to the engines, Yoel spoke:

- From what I could see during the trip, my opinion is that the MC is authorized by the Minister of the Interior, and Coco Face and his brother have to know, because they presume they know everything that happens in Cuba - commented Yoel .

"Coconut face is María Ramos's cat, who throws the stone and hides her hand," Lázaro replied.

- When the first hypocrites arrived on earth, coconut face and his brother were waiting for them, they had already made up a tall tale to get out of trouble and it was as if they didn't know anything - commented Manolo.

- They can say what they want, but the evidence indicates that they are behind everything.
Remember that coconut face is the great liar and came down from the mountains with a catholic rosary around his neck and now he is totally atheist. We sailed the entire south coast of the island, we stayed a week in Cayo Largo, administered by the National Institute of Tourism. They, who have spies everywhere, haven't they seen that? Do you really think Coconut Face (nickname for Fidel Castro) won't know? - Yoel commented.

- Don't worry kids, the movie is starting now and we're going to see something else - Lázaro finished saying.

They arrived on the island, picked up the work, and with luck on their side they crowned it all. Now it was necessary to pay part of it to the Cuban government.

Selling it was easy, it was good quality merchandise, and then came the distribution, which included taking the profit to Cuba.

The 5,100 pounds were sold at a rate of 500 dollars per pound, for a total of 2,550,000 dollars, which would be divided into 637,500 for the boatmen and 1,912,500 for the Castros.

Mayor Camejo asked for a great favor: to make some purchases to take to the island, including a yacht, which would be delivered to the MC. Camejo explained, without being asked, that it would be used for tourism.

Of the almost 2 million dollars, $250,000 would be used to buy the yacht, another $100,000 to buy various things, such as computers and personal gifts for MC officials; for example, a 15-year-old dress for so-and-so's daughter, 4 Pirelli Scorpion 255-70R16 tires for the oldest so-and-so. Also, various HP computers and Rolex and Cartier watches.

The person in charge of buying the yacht was Luis el Grande, who bought a 55-foot Defender with two Detroit 851 engines, which cost $250,000, but, in order to buy them in cash, he had had to pay $300,000, due to the danger it represented for the seller such a large transaction in cash.

Corruption has its methods and its price.

The decision was made that Yoel, Moto and Camejo would go to Cuba in the Corza boat with the money, and that Luis el Grande and Lázaro would take the Yacht with all the gifts and $1,000 in all kinds of food, especially a lot of coffee. Manolo would stay in Florida with a Mirage 36 with two Mercury 300 engines, all brand new.

There was money, and when it is like that, everything flows very well.

Yoel, Moto and Camejo left on the speedboat and were received in Varadero by other members of the Ministry of the Interior. They stayed for a few days at the Ernest Hemingway Marina in Barlovento. A week later Louis the Great and Lázaro set sail on the Defender for Marathon Key, Florida.

In their cabin they transported enough money and clothing to make thousands of Cubans happy, victims of a cruel and unjust regime. But sometimes life puts human beings in situations that they do not know how to control. If you want, you can call it selfishness, but for Lazaro, Luis, Yoel, Moto and Manolo, the game has another name: survival.

CHAPTER 5

"THE GRAY-HAIRED"

- Ojo Picho to Flaco, ojo picho to Flaco! Answer, flaco...-

The grotesque metallic sound of the 20/40 broke the silence of that placid morning in Miami. "Flaco" got up almost running from the bed and quickly grabbed the microphone of the radio that was on the other side of the room.

- Here Skinny, Ojo Picho, over! - he said, trying to hide his sleepy voice.

- What happened? We have a bird ready for the 30th, ask "Gray-haired" if we can go fishing - answered the voice calmly. And he added:-there are 5000 notebooks. -

Ojo Picho was the nickname of one of the drug traffickers who coordinated cocaine shipments from the Colombian coast to Cuba. In Miami, "Flaco", whose name we will not reveal at his request, had the task of coordinating all the protagonists of smuggling.

It was a week before the trip. - Little time. - Skinny thought.

- Understood, brother, soon I will call you with news. He replied, looking at the clock.

It was 5 in the morning.

"These people don't seem to sleep," he thought as he hung up the microphone and went back to his bed to continue sleeping. The night before he had abused a little of the white powder and it felt like his head was about to explode.

"Over and out," said the voice. The radio went silent.

Skinny went back to bed and crossed his fingers before falling asleep, praying that his mind would allow him to remember the message he had just received when he woke up in the afternoon. That job could make you a lot of money, no less than $100,000.

- Fat, here Skinny, Fat, here Skinny, do you receive me? -

30 seconds passed and a voice replied: - Skinny, Fat here, tell me. -

The "Gordo" was the person who introduced "Flaco" in the drug trafficking business. They met one day at a Miami marina and from that moment they never stopped working together. Each had an important role to play. The "Gordo" had the boats and the personnel for any type of work. In other words, he coordinated the maritime part of the smuggling. "Flaco" was the brains behind the operation. Despite his young age, barely 20 years old, he had established the contacts to achieve successful operations. He also had, on his radio, always on the lookout, the strong man of drug trafficking in Cuba: his code name was "El Canoso."

- We have a bird for the 30th, the same nest as always. 5000 notebooks - said Skinny.

The radio went silent. There was only a little static.

- Let me talk to my people, Flaco, but I don't think there's a problem. Coordinate with the "Grey-haired" to see if he can. - answered the fat man.

- Over and out - said Skinny, looking at the clock. The contact in Cuba preferred to be called during office hours, because his work was where he had the radio receiver.

It was 3:05. He changed the tune to the other frequency and pressed the microphone button.

- Skinny to Gray-haired, Skinny to Gray-haired, answers Gray-haired.-

- Skinny, it's me, Eagle, now I'm looking for it - answered a voice from the other side. The radio of his Cuban contact was not directly in Canoso's office but in an adjoining room. For strategic reasons, there was always someone waiting for the messages.

A few minutes later a firm voice, with a military tone, sounded through the small speaker.

- Skinny, here "Gray" what's new? -

- 5000 notebooks next 30th. I need confirmation. Change- explained Skinny knowing that he would not receive an immediate answer.

- So few? - Gray-haired paused and continued - Okay, I'll let you know in about 2 days, at the latest, I have a lot of movement. I don't want peos - Gray-haired said.

The amount of drugs that he used to pass through Cuba at that time was 10 to 12 thousand kilos per trip.

- As soon as possible - answered Skinny - you know, to avoid nerves. -

- It's clear, Flaco, over and out -

Gray-haired was not lying. At that time, between 1988 and 1989, Cuba had become one of the most important transit and storage points for narcotics to the United States. Not only directly, with high-speed boats entering Florida like daggers, but also lending its airspace to transit, land and store drugs for the Colombian drug czars. The island was also an important fueling bridge for aircraft and often a stopover point for cargo entering the Yuma through the Bahamas.

To coordinate such an effort, the Cubans had organized groups of men by region and task. Some were in charge of receiving the packages that fell from the sky into the water, others lowered the loads of the planes that landed on the runways of the island and those closest to "Canoso", his trusted men, were responsible for receiving the money. in cash, piles of bills that arrived weekly by boat and handed it over to him. It was almost always millions of dollars per month, you couldn't trust anyone.

Not only money was exchanged in this smuggling operation. El Gordo, who knew "el Canoso" in person, transported all kinds of merchandise to Cuba. Sometimes it was luxury watches, like Rolex, designer clothes, electronics, and even food cooked in Miami.

It is clearly documented both by the DEA, the United States anti-drug administration, the Coast Guard and the American spies in Cuba, that there was an air space where planes from Colombia constantly passed with drug shipments whose final destination was the coast of Florida. . He was called "the broker from Camagüey". Aircraft loaded with drugs flew over there day and night, with their lights on and flying low, at less than 10,000 feet, ready to unload their packages in Cadiz Bay, the precise place that Lazaro had recommended to the Cubans to deliver the contraband. . In front of this strategic place to pick up the packages and take them to the Keys, there was a Cuban border guard station that had the task of ensuring that only authorized boats entered the place to pick up the precious cargo.

These are just some of the events that demonstrate, without a doubt, the magnitude of Cuban participation in drug trafficking, only in the 1980s (source: cubacid.com):

Autumn 1981: Colombian officials declare in their country that they know that the planes that transported drugs to Cuba returned with military cargo for the guerrillas.

April 1982: Federal grand jury in Miami indicts Aldo Santamaría (head of the Cuban Navy), René Rodríguez Cruz (Director of ICAP), Fernando Ravelo, former Cuban ambassador to Colombia, and Gonzalo Bassols, second-in-command at that embassy for drug trafficking. and other MININT officials.

November 1982: Colombians and Cubans captured by the US Drug Enforcement Agency (DEA) offered a Miami court extensive evidence of Cuba's involvement in drug trafficking.

April 1983: US Undersecretary of State declared that there was evidence that since 1979 Castro had approved Cuba as a bridge for drug trafficking and a support base for drug traffickers in the US.

May 1983: President Ronald Reagan declares in Miami that "there is strong evidence that Castro officials are involved in drug trafficking and that they introduce drugs like criminals, taking advantage of the addicts' misery."

June 1983: Head of the DEA declares in the US Senate that Cuba was facilitating the movement of drugs through its territory.

July 1983: Castro intelligence deserter Jesús Raúl Méndez told US authorities that Raúl Castro accepted money from drug traffickers to use the island as a base to introduce drugs into the US.

March 1984: Colombian Minister of Defense says that the raw material enters Colombia from Bolivia and Peru and the cocaine produced is transported to Cuba by plane.

Mid-1984: After disputes with the Panamanian dictator Manuel Noriega, Castro moves the bases and laboratories from Panama to Nicaragua, as declared by the imprisoned drug trafficker in the US Carlos Lehder.

August 1984: The US Attorney General publicly accuses Cuba and Bulgaria of using drug trafficking to support terrorists. The head of the DEA insists that Cuba's participation has not ceased despite charges filed against four officials of the regime.

October 1985: Diario Las Américas (Miami) reports on a drug processing plant in Oriente, brought from East Germany. The raw material almost always arrived on the island in Cuban planes.

August 1986: Head of the US Southern Command expresses his personal conviction of Cuban involvement in drug trafficking, although Fidel Castro denied it.

April 1987: 400 kilograms of cocaine received by plane, stored in Varadero and later sent by sea to the US (as later learned in Case #1 against General Arnaldo Ochoa).

First half of 1987: The intelligence agencies of the United States already knew that "planes with drugs from Colombia were landing at the Varadero airport with the complicity of Cuban officials."

End of 1987: 500 kilograms received at the Varadero airport and transferred to three ships bound for the US (Cause #1).

January 1988: José Blandón, assistant to the Panamanian dictator Noriega, takes refuge in the US and presents documentary evidence of the participation of the Castros in drug trafficking.

February 1989: 500 kilograms dropped by plane that later landed in Varadero to refuel. Speedboats picked up and transshipped the cargo in Punta Hicacos (Cause #1).

March 1989: 400 kilograms dropped by plane near the Bay of Cádiz (Cause #1).

April 1989: A boat loaded with cocaine was repaired at the Barlovento marina (currently Marina Hemingway) and continued to Varadero to transfer the cargo in a small islet. (Cause #1).

June-July 1989: Arrest of General Arnaldo Ochoa, hero of the Republic of Cuba and member of the Central Committee of the Party, the brothers Patricio (General) and Antonio (Colonel) de la Guardia and dozens of MININT and FAR officers. Case #1 and execution of Ochoa, Tony de la Guardia and two other officers (MININT and MINFAR). The prosecutor links all of them to drug trafficking, insisting that they did so without the knowledge of the Cuban authorities. After the executions and long sentences imposed, Fidel Castro declares that he has finished drug trafficking in Cuba.

July 1989: Western diplomats in Havana report that the US Interests Section in Havana met several times with the Cuban government to discuss Castro's involvement in drug trafficking.

August 1989: Juan A. Rodríguez Menier, a deserter from the Castro intelligence, declared that Fidel Castro was personally aware of the drug business and that the CIMEX Corporation received 80% of the money generated by these operations in convertible currency.

August 1989: Case #2 against General José Abrahantes, Minister of the Interior, Pascual Martínez Gil, First Vice Minister, and a dozen MININT officers. Twenty years in prison for Abrahantes, twelve for Martínez Gil, and shorter sentences for the rest.

These news headlines are only a small fraction of all the events that implicate the Cuban government with drug trafficking. In his article "El Cartel de la Habana" the late writer Carlos J. Bringuier writes:

"There are numerous examples of how the Castro brothers created the Havana Cartel. There is the case of Reynaldo Ruiz and his son Rubén. Reynaldo Ruiz had connections in Cuba through a relative, Miguel Ruiz, who was a Captain in the Ministry of the Interior.

"Reinaldo Ruiz was a naturalized North American from Havana. He was not a communist, much less a supporter of the Fidel Castro regime. But the magnitude of the business and the common benefits that he would contribute, allowed him to ignore those differences and show himself with his cousin in the best disposition to reach an agreement. The Cubans would only have to authorize their planes to land in Varadero and transfer the drugs to Punta Hicacos, where their *cigarette boats* would wait. Commissions for those services would be substantial." (excerpt from an article written by Daniel Iglesias Kennedy for Nostalgia Cuba).

According to what Reynaldo Ruiz declared, he was traveling to Cuba on a boat from Florida arriving in Varadero where he was waiting for his son Rubén, who was in Colombia. His son was flying from Colombia to Varadero on a plane loaded with cocaine, a Colonel of the Cuban Air Force authorized Rubén's flight to Cuba. Rubén landed in Varadero and it seemed as if his flight was a routine thing and they gave him a succulent lunch while the Cuban military unloaded the cocaine and transferred it to Reynaldo's boat. Already with the boat loaded, a Cuban coast guard escorted them to the high seas.

Reynaldo Ruiz and his son were arrested in Miami in 1988. As the Castro brothers' collusion with the drug mafia was yet to be discovered, the Castro government denied the accusations and proceeded to look for scapegoats. Subsequently Arnaldo Ochoa (Hero of the Revolution), Tony de La Guardia (Fidel Castro's personal friend), Captain Miguel Ruiz (Reynaldo Ruiz's relative), as well as 11 other people were arrested and subjected to summary trial. When Captain Miguel Ruiz said during his statement that he had the impression that the drug operation was approved at the "maximum level", Prosecutor Juan Escalona asked to suspend the trial for a few minutes since, according to Escalona, the defendant was very nervous. Captain Miguel Ruiz did not return to continue his statement.

Previously, planes loaded with drugs from Colombia had to pass over Cuban airspace and none of those planes were shot down like the Brothers to the Rescue plane. The drug cartels obtained in advance, for a fee, authorization from the Castro government to fly over the necessary airspace to offload their deadly cargo over the Bahamas.

Another involved in this smuggling turned out to be George Morales who testified in Washington that he participated in the movement of drugs through Cuba. Morales testified that this occurred from 1980 to 1986.

Jack Blum was the Senate Special Prosecutor (1987-1989). The main witness was José Blandón, a former assistant to Manuel Noriega who declared that he had attended meetings in Cuba with Fidel Castro, presenting photographs to prove it.

Blandón assured that the Cubans were involved in drug trafficking and that Castro's motives "are political." Blandón accused Cuba of transferring drugs through Nicaragua and Panama in addition to Colombia and that everything was directed by the Department of Latin America, the Cuban government and sponsored by Fidel Castro. The America Department had been created in 1974 and Manuel Piñeiro Losada was in charge of directing it."

In a book written by alias "Popeye", a famous Colombian hitman who became Pablo Escobar's right-hand man, he points out that "his boss was happy with that route (Colombia-Cuba-United States). He said that it was a pleasure doing business with Raúl Castro, because he was a serious and enterprising man."

According to Velásquez, the operation to which he refers, which lasted two years, was conducted "by the Cuban military under the command of General (Arnaldo) Ochoa and officer Tony de la Guardia, under direct instructions from Raúl Castro."

The operation in Cuba was carried out through planes that transported between 10,000 and 12,000 kilograms of cocaine on each flight. According to "Popeye" it was so successful that it allowed Escobar to considerably multiply his earnings.

For each kilo of cocaine transported to Florida, the Cuban government received $2,000 and $200 if they only guarded it, that is, they kept it in their possession until someone picked it up. Doing the math, if each plane brought 10 to 12 thousand kilos of drugs, Cubans earned between 20 and 24 million dollars per load. 2 to 2.4 million for taking care of her for a certain time, according to Popeye.

And now, thanks to the testimonies collected for this book, much more is known about the Cuba-Colombia connection. Until now, it had only been said that the cocaine shipments came almost exclusively from the Medellín Cartel, led by the bloodthirsty leader Pablo Escobar. Both El Flaco and Yoel and Lazaro testify that two other organizations took advantage of the easy access to the southern coasts of the United States and the efficiency of the Cubans who moved the product. They are the Cali Cartel, of the Rodriguez Orejuela brothers, and the Coastal Cartel, commanded by José Rafael Abello Silva, alias "Mono Abello".

"Ojo Picho", the intermediary who contacted Skinny on the radio at the beginning of this chapter, along with two others named "Juancho" and "Edgar", were all members of the Coastal Cartel.

These criminal groups, responsible for the entry of thousands of tons of drugs into the United States, had direct contact with the Cuban government to coordinate shipments, commissions and solve any problem that might arise during the transit of the drug from Colombia to the Cuban shores.

Why had all these organizations and the Cuban government organized themselves to carry out these risky operations? Simple: the profits were fabulous. If in a month they could move 100 tons of cocaine, they could easily clean 2 billion dollars.

El Flaco does not doubt for a second that all those drug trafficking operations that were carried out in different regions of the country were organized and coordinated from the highest levels of government. He is not the only one who thinks that nothing moves in Cuba without the consent of Fidel and his brother. Anyone who has lived on the island knows this perfectly well. But El Flaco has very solid proof that this is so. And it is that "El Canoso", the man with whom he spoke to coordinate all the shipments, the person who told him where, how and when to move the drug, was, no other, than Division General José Abrahantes Fernandez , Minister of the Interior of Cuba from 1985 to 1989.

CHAPTER 6

ABRANTES

- General, the commander is on the phone. -

The voice on the intercom sounded urgent. But who would feel normal after hearing Fidel Castro himself?

- Jose, how are you? How's the family? asked the unmistakable sound.

Abrahantes froze, what he least imagined was hearing such a cordial greeting from the man who, according to what they told him, wanted to put him in jail for treason.

"Very well, my commander," he managed to say, trying to hide his anguish. - Ivan, Lilly and Juan Carlos always ask me about you. Let's see when we can meet.

Abrahantes knew perfectly well what his interlocutor was capable of. He still had fresh in his memory the news of the shooting of two of his powerful friends, General Ochoa and Colonel De la Guardia, which had occurred a few months earlier. So he tried to buy a little compassion and sympathy from the man he feared so much, especially in this time of change and uncertainty.

- Soon we will, we have to let the storm pass, dear friend, I am very busy with international issues and there is hardly any rest, but as soon as possible, we meet. Castro said without a single hint of hypocrisy in his voice.

The Cuban Minister of the Interior had the worst of premonitions. Castro was saying goodbye, his way. After all, we had spent a lot of time together. Abrahantes was, for many years, his chief escort.

Even saving his life too many times wasn't going to prevent the inevitable. Fidel Castro holds a Guinness record for assassination attempts, with more than 680, and during the years that Abrahantes was his personal protector, there were several, all failed.

- To what do I owe the honor of your call, commander? -I manage to say while hundreds of ideas went through his mind.

-No, nothing, I just wanted to say hello, someone told me that he saw you recently and I remembered that we have a pending talk about the course of the revolution. Castro explained.

Abrahantes's face changed color, from red to white in a second. His boss's words sounded treacherous.

Suddenly the office door opened and 4 men dressed in green interrupted the conversation. Abrahantes managed to get up and immediately remembered that his possible savior was on the phone.

-Commander-he said hastily-what is happening?

The line went silent.

The highest-ranking officer came up with handcuffs in his hand and said, as he put them on:

- Division General Jose Abrahantes Fernandez, is under arrest for treason. He come with us.

- Who ordered this? - I manage to ask, despite knowing the answer.

More silence.

The 3 soldiers surrounded him to escort him to the vehicle waiting outside. The subordinates who worked for Abrahantes in the MININT or Ministry of the Interior of Cuba watched in silence as their boss of so many years walked out in handcuffs. Most understood that this was the last time they would see him in the building.

Abrahantes pretended not to understand what was happening, but he knew perfectly well the magnitude of his problem. In July of that same year, just 2 months earlier, the head of the MC, one of its most valuable dependencies, Colonel Tony De la Guardia, had fallen under the bullets of a firing squad after a trial considered by many as a mocks justice and intelligence. That same day Fidel Castro had got rid of his main imaginary opponent, General Arnaldo Ochoa, considered a hero of the revolution, protagonist of an epic campaign in Angola, where he received important awards for his victories in favor of the Cuban cause. .

If Castro was able to have 2 of his most faithful collaborators shot, nothing would stop him from doing the same to him.

Abrahantes recalled, on the way to his destination, all the meetings he had had with him and his brother Raul to coordinate drug trafficking to the United States. He also knew that this matter was the biggest state secret that existed at that time in Cuba. Revealing it would be a huge stain on the reputation of the Revolution, in a country hit by a brutal US embargo that seriously affected its economy, although at the same time it served the propaganda purposes of the regime.

Jose "Pepe" Abrahantes was one of the most powerful characters of the moment. Son of an old and powerful militant of the Cuban Communist Party. He went into exile in Mexico very young, when fighting against Fulgencio Batista. Pepe was very organized and had a gentle, chivalrous personality and very correct manners. Patient man, observant and very balanced. He was put to work with Castro on the recommendation of his father.

He was so involved with the "Comandante" that some joked that he was the best "crazy" in Cuba. On the other hand, he was a man who calmly, coolly made big decisions and executed them with flying colors. He was a very discreet person in his public and private life. A born psychologist, calculating and with a quick mind.

The promise of huge profits through drug trafficking gave Fidel Castro and his brother the final push to launch a plan that would generate billions of dollars: take advantage of the short distance between the Cuban coast and the Florida Keys. to enter thousands of tons of marijuana and cocaine, as well as any other drug that the Colombian drug lords want to send.

The hatred that the Castros felt for his nemesis was also enough reason to want to get into this dirty and lucrative business. Fidel Castro always expressed his desire to destroy the United States from the outside or from the inside. Since the Soviet missile crisis did not fulfill its macabre objective, it was time to do it from within, poisoning the population of it.

Pablo Escobar and the Rodriguez Orejuela brothers, as well as representatives of several smaller Colombian cartels, had visited the island on many occasions seeking to conquer this easy access route to the United States. Offers began to pour in at the end of the 1970s. There was supply and demand, the perfect scenario to start the bombardment of illegal drugs to the richest country in the world.

All the Castros had to do was say yes. The rest, the operational part, was simple, they had an entire army at their disposal, servile and indoctrinated people, perfect for carrying out a plan of such enormous magnitude.

And that was precisely what they did. Little by little, with trials and errors, the Castro Cartel was born.

However, this included keeping the greatest of secrets. Drug smuggling was to remain a covert operation; no one could ever know that the Castro brothers were involved.

The origin of the Castro Cartel dates back to the end of the 1970s. It all started, according to witnesses and press articles, when Fabio Vásquez Castaño, head of the Colombian insurgent movement M-19, managed to establish contact with Manuel Piñero. Losada (Barbarossa), director of the America Department, the intelligence section of the Cuban Communist Party. Vásquez Castaño proposed a business that consisted of acquiring weapons from Cuba and paying for them with cocaine. Piñero Losada presented the idea to his superiors, emphasizing that drugs were a destabilizing element in the United States government and society. At the same time, cocaine was the equivalent of convertible currency and on the other hand it helped the Colombian rebels in their attacks against democracy in Colombia and the rest of the region.

The business was approved.

Then the need arose to create a system to convert the drug into dollars. It had to be sold elsewhere since Fidel Castro would never allow the presence of drugs on the island. The solution was simple: they had the richest country on the planet 90 miles away, you didn't have to be a scientist to do that equation. It was only necessary to get someone to put it on North American soil, there were groups of drug traffickers who would be in charge of selling it without problems.

Round business.

In one of Fidel Castro's conversations with General Abrahantes, he clearly told him that "if any smuggling operation was discovered and his involvement was suspected, he should take all the blame and pay the price."

Abrahantes, of course, accepted the "order" of his boss, as he had done all his life.

There are ample testimonies of many witnesses who defected to the United States and give credence to the illegal activities of the Castro brothers and their lieutenants.

Juan Reinaldo Sánchez was one of the members of the security ring of the Cuban President. He tells in his book "The Hidden Life of Fidel Castro" that one day in 1988, he overheard a conversation between Fidel Castro and General José Abrahantes.

"Fidel was directing cocaine trafficking like a true godfather. It was a tremendous shock. I felt used. I had wanted to give my life for a man who was a drug trafficker," says Sánchez, who died in exile in Miami in 2015. Until that moment for this bodyguard "Fidel Castro was a god".

Colombian drug trafficker Carlos Lehder, who was released from a US prison in 2020 after serving a third of his 125-year sentence for drug trafficking, told a British media outlet that the Cuban government allowed planes carrying cocaine shipments from Colombia to make a stopover. on the Caribbean island to refuel and then continue the route to the United States.

Channel 4 of England, in its program "Dispatches" investigated the case and interviewed a former agent of the Cuban secret services, who said he had personally seen Fidel Castro order the creation of a company dedicated to covering up drug trafficking.

He was undoubtedly referring to the aforementioned MC, an agency dependent on the MININT, in charge of Colonel Antonio de la Guardia, one of those shot by Castro in 1989.

Dispatches highlight that many members of the Cuban Army were used by the Medellín Cartel to help transport up to six tons of cocaine from planes to ships bound for the United States, with a street value of about 150 million dollars during a year and a half period.
According to evidence collected by Dispatches, up to fifteen boats per week had been involved in these drug trafficking operations.

On the other hand, former Cuban general Rafael del Pino declared, once he arrived in exile in Miami, that he often received instructions from Raúl Castro, Fidel's brother, to allow planes from Colombia to land in Cuba.

Everyone agrees that Castro's goal was to use drug trafficking in his war strategy against US imperialism and to obtain foreign currency. Many of the members of the army also believed that, in a war against imperialism, it was valid to use any kind of trick to weaken the United States.

When Abrahantes arrived at the Government Palace, handcuffed and escorted like a criminal, he realized that his fate was sealed.

The day Fidel Castro removed his protection, he knew from experience after what happened to him a few months ago, he would become a criminal in the eyes of Cubans and the world. And that day he had arrived. Now what he had to try to do was avoid being shot, like Ochoa and De la Guardia, two of his colleagues and friends.

Much had changed since his former boss exploded with fury because of international pressure when his involvement in drug trafficking was discovered. Fidel Castro used to meet with Abrahantes often to discuss, among other things, the ins and outs of the lucrative drug business.

Image: one of the few photos that exist of General Abrahantes with Fidel Castro.

In his cell at the Palace of the Revolution, waiting to learn of his fate, the now deposed Minister of the Interior recalled several conversations he had with Castro just a few months earlier.

- Jose, we have a serious problem, the Colombian planes that land on our runways take a long time to get in and out. I have received reports that this can be detected by gringos and must be avoided at all costs. Also, sometimes, we don't have fuel to give them. Do you think you could solve that problem? Fidel said with a calm and slightly low voice, to avoid being heard by his assistants and bodyguards from outside the office.

His aides have said on several occasions that when no voices were heard in the Commander in Chief's office, it was because they were talking about drug trafficking. This, however, did not prevent several conversations between Castro, Abrahantes and De la Guardia from being heard where the drug issue was touched upon.

- My Commander, I have been thinking about it, we need to find a place where they can launch the packages, that is safe and where nobody can steal it or that they do not end up floating out to sea and get lost. Abrahantes suggested.

- Steal? How can that be possible? No Cuban would dare to do it right under our noses. - Castro replied, trying to keep his voice calm.

- Don't forget, Commander, that many boatmen come to our shores carrying merchandise to Miami. If they came across some packages floating on the shore, who knows what they might do. - Abrahantes explained trying to show efficiency.

Castro leaned back in his presidential chair and thought for a moment. In his right hand rested the most emblematic symbol of his image: a cigar. He brought it to his mouth and a puff of smoke covered his shrewd, tired eyes for a moment.

- It always has to be a protected place, but we cannot have a boat there 24 hours a day, the best thing is to find a place in front of a border guard or marine station. And also keep in mind that not everyone knows about these activities, the commander must be one of ours. - Fidel said before taking the cigarette back to his mouth. Smoke filled the space for a few seconds. The smell of tobacco bothered Abrahantes a lot, a man who loved a healthy life, who did not like vices. However, for many years, as head of security for the Cuban president, he had become accustomed to such an atrocity for the senses.

- I know what we'll do. -said the minister pretending that he had enjoyed that smoke on his face- I am going to ask one of my contacts in Miami if he knows an expert in maritime cartography who can guide us. They have worked with us for a long time and will have no problem helping us.

- But how, we don't have anyone who knows about the subject? - Castro asked with surprise.

- Not to my knowledge, Commander, the Cuban boatmen from Miami have always been the experts on the Cuban coast. Maybe you can ask one of our sailors, but it would take a lot of time and it's best to keep everything as discreet as possible. It is better to play it safe. Abrahantes replied, almost murmuring, leaning towards Castro and therefore towards his cigar. He tried to hide the look of disgust on his face.

- Do that, comrade, get a worm that knows. - Fidel smiled briefly and waved goodbye to Abrahantes, who got up and left the office unhurriedly. Every time he met with Castro he was reminded of the times he thought he would give his life for that man. Soon, that macabre thought would come true, under strange circumstances.

The memory was interrupted by the sound of the cell door opening. Two guards accompanied him to an office where they made him wait for more than half an hour, time that Abrahantes used to fervently hope that it was all a misunderstanding.

Several soldiers, with folders in their hands, interrupted their prayers and sat down in front of him.

A colonel, in charge of the military justice department, read him the accusations: abuse in office, negligence in service, improper use of material and financial resources, bribery, misappropriation, and ignorance about the illegal activities that allegedly "in an unauthorized" was committed by several officers under his command.

Undoubtedly, Fidel Castro had unleashed all his fury against his former friend and confidante. And Abrahantes knew that it would be impossible to tell the truth, that the man he had protected for so long was, in fact, the mastermind behind a multi-million dollar drug operation. He would not tell the truth for the safety of his children and his family. He also did not want to suffer the same fate as his friends, General Ochoa and Colonel De la Guardia.

And so it was, during his trial he limited himself to answering questions from the military prosecutor and trying to minimize the damage as much as possible. The Cuban government, in a strange attitude of media openness, posted an edited version of Abrahantes' trial on YouTube for the world to see. There you can clearly see the attitude of resignation of the former head of the MININT in the face of questions that he could easily have answered with "Fidel asked me, ordered me or told me." However, he chose to keep quiet and accept his fate.

In one of the accusations, he was questioned about the acquisition of a fleet of 1,200 modern cars that were used by ministry personnel. Abrahantes responded that he had bought them using a "special" fund that he could access from his position as boss. It is believed that this money, some 3 million dollars, came from drug trafficking and that the Castros were aware of every movement of money, especially considering that, to enter imported vehicles on a large scale, it was necessary to involve many officials. of the Cuban government, such as customs, ONAT (National Office of Tax Administration), the Ministry of Finance and the Ministry of Foreign Trade. It is absolutely impossible for Abrahantes to be able to make a million-dollar purchase of automobiles without the hierarchs of the Cuban Communist Party knowing about it. Not in Cuba, that is completely impossible.

The Castro Cartel functioned like many other organizations dedicated to drug trafficking. It had an indisputable, powerful and cruel leader, Fidel, and his right-hand man, Raul, then Minister of the Armed Forces, made decisions when his brother was absent or they simply weren't that important. Directly below them was General Jose Abrahantes Fernandez, Minister of the Interior, who had under his control thousands of soldiers willing to do whatever was necessary to help the revolution, as well as vehicles, installations, and weapons.

To channel all the illegal activities in a single place, the cartel bosses created the MC, a division of the MININT that was in charge of organizing everything related to circumventing the blockade, either by generating foreign currency through illicit business in Panama or coordinating drug trafficking from Colombia to the United States, with a stopover in Cuba. This office was in charge of Colonel Antonio de la Guardia and was dismantled shortly before his death, in July 1989. Everything that entered Cuba for the MC did not go through any Customs control.

Beneath this dome were hundreds of officers from the Cuban army, navy, air force, and border guard. Men and women who were born and raised within the revolution, and who would never dare to dispute an order from their superiors, however illegal it may be.

In this story we have named some of the members of the Castro Cartel: Major Sánchez Lima, second-in-command in the MC, Colonel Ramon Blanco, chief of the Matanzas province border, and Captain Hermes Rivero, also a member of the MC. Major Camejo, who personally accompanied a drug shipment to Florida, also operated under the command of Colonel De la Guardia.

Another participant, although not as active in the drug trafficking operations themselves, was Air Force General Rafael del Pino, who reports having received several times direct orders from Raul Castro and Abrahantes to allow planes loaded with drugs to pass over the island, over Cuban airspace.

Del Pino defected from Cuba in 1987 and began to tell all the media in great detail about his participation in the cartel's operations.

- Several times I received orders from the office of Raúl Castro and also from the office of General Abrantes to let the plane cross Cuba. he told PBS's Frontline.

INTERVIEWER: -Now, what kind of orders did he receive?

Gen. Del PINO: - Simply, "Tomorrow at 2:00 p.m. Zulu is going to pilot a plane like this one, with two engines. Let them fly."

According to the General, the planes often traversed some of the most restricted airspace in the country.

Gen. Del PINO: - In the western part of Cuba, we have 19 SAM missile sites, hundreds of radars, and a regiment of MiG-23 interceptors. It is completely impossible for a small plane to fly from Colombia to the United States without the knowledge and permission of the Cuban authority.

According to del Pino, the military high command assumed that drugs were part of state policy. The officers even discussed the rights and wrongs of it.

- Everybody knew that they were getting into this business. Some of them were against it and some were for it. Some say it was foul play and others say, 'Well, in this kind of war against the imperialists, we can use all our tricks and the Ultimate Leader knows the weak part of the United States and this is the way to make them weaker'. In Cuba, more than in other totalitarian countries, nothing moves without the knowledge of Fidel Castro. -

From time to time, and to "demonstrate" that the Cuban government was actively fighting drug trafficking, the official press published on the front page the destruction of drug shipments confiscated from drug traffickers. The chronicle reported that the drugs were incinerated in the ovens of the steel company Antillana de Acero, located in the municipality of Cotorro, near Havana.

Actually, the "confiscated" drug shipments, which were actually drugs that they had to transport and trade, were housed in special warehouses of the Ministry of the Interior. What they burned, in reality, were packages of waste. The person in charge of supervising the operation was Lieutenant Colonel Rosal, married to a daughter of the head of Cuban intelligence: Ramiro Valdez, a close friend of the Castro brothers and Abrahantes.

The real drug was transported on a Cuban Navy ship, under the command of Vice Admiral Aldo Santamaría Cuadrado, who delivered it to boatmen from Miami at strategic points in the northern keys of Cuba or in Cayo Largo del Sur.

Vice Admiral Aldo Santamaría Cuadrado with Raul Castro

On several occasions, Colombian drug traffickers "bombed" the drug in 2 different places in Cuba: one was the shipment to take to Miami, the other, the payment, in merchandise" for the members of the Cartel. The commission for facilitating the transport of the drug from Colombia to the United States was arranged in advance, but it used to vary between 20 and 25% of the total shipment, which added up to hundreds of millions of dollars each month. The extra cargo was delivered to Miami boatmen to be sold in South Florida and then they took the money and other material goods to Cuba. The boats used to come loaded with food, appliances, Rolex and Cartier watches, as well as tires for imported cars on the island. Those in charge of receiving the money, in most cases, were Colonel De la Guardia and General Abrahantes.

In 1982, the United States government indicted 14 Cubans for drug trafficking, including four high-ranking officials of the Government and the Central Committee of the Communist Party of Cuba, accused of charges related to the importation of methaqualone tablets and marijuana into the United States. The drugs came from Colombia and arrived in Florida through Cuba. The Cuban officials were accused of acts specifically designed to facilitate the importation of drugs and circumvent US interdiction efforts.

They were: Fernando Ravelo Renedo, the Cuban ambassador in Colombia; Gonzalo Bassols Suarez, Minister Counselor of the Embassy of Cuba in Colombia; Aldo Santamaria Cuadrado also known as René Baeza Rodríguez, member of the Central Committee of the Communist Party of Cuba, who also held the rank of Vice Admiral of the Cuban Navy; and, finally, René Rodríguez Cruz, member of the Central Committee, also, of the Communist Party of Cuba and president of the Cuban Institute of Friendship with the People, also known as ICAP. None were tried in North American prisons.

Other Cubans belonging to the Castro Cartel were arrested and served sentences for drugs in the United States in the 1980s and 1990s. They are José Domingo Martínez, Alberto Cortez, Cornelio Ramos Valladares, David Lorenzo Pérez, Jorge Felipe Llerena Delgado, Jose Rafael Martinez and Hector Gonzalez.

These are just samples of the magnitude of this organization. There is no doubt that in Cuba it would have been impossible to mount such a large operation without Fidel and his brother Raul knowing about it. For so many members of the Communist Party it would have been impossible to keep such a secret, much less for so many years. Also, everyone knows that betraying the Grand Commander would have tragic consequences for whoever dared.

Fidel Castro himself acknowledged, after the trial of General Ochoa and Colonel De la Guardia, that between 1985 and 1988 more than 3 tons of cocaine had passed through the island bound for the United States. This admission had the purpose of blaming those convicted for their participation in drug trafficking and, incidentally, acknowledging their existence, but in reality it is known that there were many more than 3, thousands of tons, and each and every one, with their full knowledge. .

That is why Castro felt the need to shoot his former comrades and friends, to clear his file before the world and show everyone that he was the victim of his subordinates and not his boss. They had warned him from high international circles that if he continued along this path he could provoke a direct North American intervention on the island, like what happened years later to Manuel Noriega in Panama. And that could not be allowed. The United States would never dare to overthrow a dictator, but it would arrest a drug lord.

As revealed by Popeye, Colombian drug trafficker Pablo Escobar's lieutenant, in his memoirs, the Colombian capo convinced Fidel Castro to participate in drug trafficking to Florida not only because of the enormous profits that this business would generate but also because he made him see that drugs bound for the United States were a destabilizing element of the government and society of that country.

Fidel consulted his brother Raúl de el, and both agreed to use drug trafficking as historical revenge against the North American empire. But not to forget the enormous profits generated by this business, estimated at billions of dollars for the coffers of the Castros.

One of the Cubans who testified in a US court in the 1980s said that during a drug smuggling operation he met a Cuban government official named Rene Cruz. He told him that Fidel Castro himself traveled through Central and South America doing all kinds of things related to drug trafficking and that he was happy that they took the drugs to the United States through Cuba. Castro said, very seriously, that they could take Florida any time they felt like it.

That's right, invading the United States while its inhabitants were drugged. Castro's words.

This is the same man who, since the triumph of his revolution more than 60 years ago, has claimed higher morals. Castro said that drugs, like gambling and prostitution, were eliminated in Cuba when they took power. However, the truth is plain to see, it is enough to visit Cuba to realize that it is a desperate country, where women, including professionals, sell their bodies in order to eat and feed their children.

I have seen it with my own eyes, girls, boys, women and men of all ages, offer themselves to tourists like flies in the manure, at the exit of the hotels. There is no food, no cleaning supplies, soap or towels. Several times, young boys of about 12 years approached me during my trip asking me to give them towels or soaps from the hotel. I heard about an acquaintance who had sex with a 15-year-old girl in exchange for buying her a Barbie. That is the Cuba that Castro cannot claim, the cruel and unjust monster that he created and built with his lies, the Frankenstein of the Caribbean.

The arrest in Miami of Cuban drug trafficker Reinaldo Ruiz and his son Ruben put the Cuban government in a bind. His confessions blew her cover. Cuba no longer had denial and many of the members of the Cartel were exposed, especially their leaders.

This is how the writer Juan F. Benemelis describes these events in his article called "El Cartel de la Habana":

"In 1988 the band had been infiltrated by North American secret agents who posed as buyers and managed to audio and video record their interviews. Father and son appear in the video telling an undercover DEA agent how Cuba guaranteed the transit of cocaine shipments through the island. Ruiz is heard talking about what Castro had to be paid.

The file recounts in detail two occasions in which Rubén Ruiz had flown from Colombia to the Varadero military airport with 500 kilos of cocaine each time. On the first occasion of Ruiz's visit to Cuba in April 1987, the drug had been unloaded by military personnel and then transported to a dock and loaded onto a ship named Florida, which was escorted by Cuban Coast Guardsmen until it left the territorial waters. On May 9, Ruiz made another similar flight during which his cocaine-laden plane was escorted by a Cuban MiG until it landed at the Varadero airport. In one of the recorded conversations, it is stated verbatim that the money from this latest shipment had ended up in the hands of Castro.

In the recordings, it was discovered how the Cuban border guard service monitored the straits between the island and Florida, to ensure that traffickers could evade US patrol boats. It was also documented how the Cuban Air Force and Coast Guard provided protection to the traffickers who carried out the transfer of the drug at points on the Island for its remission to the United States."

After the pot was uncovered, one of the most affected was Colonel Antonio de la Guardia.

-He was very lonely and it was like a fog. He didn't know where to go. - said Jose Luis Llovio-Menendez, a former employee of the Ministry of Finance who was a relative of the head of the MC.

-The last week of May 1989 he called me and told me that he was involved in drug trafficking along with José Abrahantes, and Fidel was the one who gave Abrahantes orders.

Llovio-Menendez says that he was very upset with the news.

- How can you get involved in something like that? he asked her.

- It was an order without an alternative. - De la Guardia replied on the verge of tears - I had to do it. And I know that if something happens, I will be alone. If this is known, I will be alone and no one will protect me. -

During his court martial, De la Guardia knew that many of those present had direct knowledge of the drug operations. Some had even participated in them. But no one would speak in his defense.

Admiral Santamaría was one of those who signed De la Guardia's sentence, although he himself participated in drug trafficking and is one of the many members of the Cuban government accused of drug trafficking in United States courts.

Tony de la Guardia knew that Fidel was directly involved in drug trafficking. He knew too much, that's why he had to get rid of him.
Here is another anecdote that relates the Commander to drug trafficking: witnesses say that on August 13, in one of the residences on Havana's Tarará beach, relatives and close friends of Fidel Castro were celebrating his birthday.

Attendees had given him antiques and weapons, among other things; José Abrahantes arrived with a suitcase full of dollars from the dirty business of the Ministry of the Interior, and when handing it to Castro, he comments with a smile: "a few dollars for the Revolution." Fidel thanked him with a hug and handed it to Pepín Naranjo, the Comandante's private accountant.

This close friendship and complicity between the two did not help the former Minister of the Interior when it came to sealing his fate.

After an absolutely indefensible trial, Major General Jose Abrahantes Fernandez was found guilty of all the charges against him and sentenced to 20 years in prison by a military court, with the absolute certainty that the verdict had the blessing and approval of the commander in chief.

He was not shot, but in 1991, according to sources close to the general, the Castro government took away the medicine he was taking for high blood pressure and Abrahantes died a few days later of cardiac arrest in prison.

He had just served a year and a few months of his sentence.

Thus, Fidel Castro got rid of another obstacle in his march towards the sad historical feat of governing more than half a century oppressing an entire nation. He was also unable to keep the promise he had made to doctor Juan Abrahantes, after whom the University of Havana stadium is named, when he told him that he would take care of his brother José de el.

Castro's lies are widely documented throughout his life; he built his doctrine on lies, and that this was just one of them.

Trying to clean up his image in front of the world, Fidel Castro appeared on local television a short time later, proclaiming that "Yankee imperialism failed in its attempts to tarnish the image of the Cuban Revolution with drug trafficking."

Another of her thousands of lies.

The reality is that today, the body of General Jose Abrahantes Fernandez is buried, without honors, in the Colon Cemetery, in the heart of Havana.

CHAPTER 7

THE MEETING IN CUBA

The boat was rapidly approaching the newcomers, who were patiently waiting on the stopped boat at the entrance to the Bay of Cardenas. She was a 27 foot Cabin Cruiser with two inboard engines. Inside it, two Cuban soldiers stood out in their traditional olive green uniform and another man in civilian clothes. It would soon become known that all three were members of the Castro Cartel.

Waiting for them for a long time, anchored and unable to move, was the "Ali Baba", without the 40 thieves, a 52-foot "defender" type lobster boat that carries 1000 gallons of oil, with 2 Caterpillar 3208 engines. The warehouse held thousands of dollars in gifts and two crew members who had come to fulfill a mission at the request of the Cuban Ministry of the Interior.

As the Cuban delegation approached, it could be seen that they were not simple fishermen or tourists on the high seas. She was undoubtedly a government ship, on an official mission.

Lázaro, as soon as he saw them, he commented to Luis, his companion: -these are the people of "Cara de Coco", because nothing on that island moves without them knowing it.-

Luis Rodriguez was no rookie when it came to international intrigue. Luis "el Grande", as he was called because of his great height, had worked for the CIA and they called him "piece of cake" because everything seemed easy to him.

- Are you the companions of the internationalist mission? - said Major Sánchez Lima, second in command of the Cuban MC and the only one who came dressed in street clothes.

- Yes, it's us - Luis replied.

For military personnel interacting with strangers on a highly secret mission, the three men seemed very calm. Some would say professionals, others who seemed to have everything under control.

Sánchez Lima, visibly in command of the operation, ordered: - Come with us. -

The two ships headed for land.

The soldiers accompanying Sánchez Lima were Colonel Ramon Blanco, head of the Matanzas province border, and Captain Hermes Rivero, also a member of the MC, a division of the Cuban Ministry of the Interior created by the government of Fidel Castro to circumvent the embargo and acquire technology from the United States through shell companies abroad. The main headquarters of this deception was Panama City where the Cuban Revolution had created hundreds of false identities that operated as independent companies destined to generate dollars and acquire everything that was necessary to keep a weak and troubled government afloat. internal.

As they headed toward the dock, Lázaro felt relieved. They were about to reach dry land, successfully. It is that this trip had begun full of complications for the two North American residents. If they had been superstitious, perhaps this trip would never have happened because of all the signs that the universe offered them.

The Ali Baba's rudder had broken down the day before, when they were already sailing to Cuba. The pump that allowed him to operate the rudder had lost all its liquid and, without being able to turn to the right or left, it was impossible to set course towards his final destination.

They realized the problem as soon as they passed near the Sombrero lighthouse, a point of reference widely used by Lázaro and other expert sailors, especially if they are dedicated to drug trafficking. It is located off the coast of Marathon Island, in the Florida Keys, south of the Seven Mile Bridge.

- Captain - said Luis with a frightened face - the rudder of the ship does not govern.

Lázaro went to check and saw that, indeed, the rudder had lost the liquid from the pump.

- For Cuba we have 70 miles left that we cannot do without a rudder. We have no choice but to return and fix it-he said.

- But how are we going to return without a rudder? Louis asked.

- Very easy, we are going to do it with the motors, just like driving a tank with the tracks, speed is given to the motor on the right and the boat turns to the right, speed is given to the motor on the left and the boat turns left.

Following Lázaro's instructions, they managed to reach the dock and moor the Ali Baba. As soon as they were on land, Manolo, the mechanic who always got them out of trouble, went to work to fix the rudder and they took advantage of the unexpected stop to add oil again.

It was time to leave again, it was getting very late and the crew was afraid that the Cubans would get tired of waiting or that, not knowing about them, they would simply abort the mission.

But if the beginning of this adventure was bumpy, things were about to get worse. The sea decided to show its temperament and in a matter of minutes they realized that the wind had changed and was now blowing very strongly.

- Shall we go like this? - he asked Louis.

"We're leaving like this," Lázaro replied.

At 9 p.m. the Ali Baba was 180 degrees, that is, frank south, and at 20 miles per hour. By midnight they had already left the Sombrero lighthouse behind, sailing with a sea of furious waves. At dawn they were in front of Cayo Mono in front of Varadero.

Lázaro picked up the VHF radio on channel 10 and spoke in a firm voice.

- Galician for the great, Galician for the great, forward Galician.

Be quiet.

"Galician for the big one, Galician for the big one, go ahead Galician," he repeated.

Any.

- Neither Galician, nor Asturian, nor Andalusian. No one answers - Lázaro said frustrated but more than anything worried.

- We are going to enter the Bay of Cárdenas - recommended Luis.

- That bay is very dangerous. It has a lot of bass and a lot of stone. We are going to try to stay here and see with whom we can send a message to the Cuban border guards - Lázaro replied.

They didn't have to wait long. Fortunately, shortly after, a small boat with several fishermen passed by them. Luis made a sign with his hand and the fishermen approached.

- Comrades, can you please go to the border guard's base and tell him that the internationalists they are waiting for are already here.

As every favor must be accompanied by a reward, Lázaro gave him 4 packages of Pilón coffee and some frog legs. 20 minutes later the welcoming committee made its appearance.

Already sailing within the Bay of Cárdenas, Luis took the floor:

-I'm already believing that this is authorized by "Cara de Coco" himself and his brother.

- Can not it be any other way. He has control of the Navy, the Ministry of Tourism and the Border Guard forces. In a country where everyone watches everyone, it cannot be otherwise that they have the authorization of "Cara de Coco" himself - Lázaro replied.

If you are still wondering who "Cara de Coco" is, they are referring to Fidel Castro.

The two boats arrived next to a ship anchored in the center of the Bay of Cárdenas and the yacht, after placing the defenses, was moored next to it.

- Jump on the boat, why don't you go with us! - Mayor Sánchez yelled at them from the boat.

With the speed of age, in a two by three Luis and Lázaro were on Siboney's deck.

One of the crew members asked Luis:

- Is there any merchandise on the yacht?

- The warehouse is full.- Luis answered quickly.

- And for whom is what comes on the yacht? - the soldier asked again.

- I guess it's for you - Lázaro replied.

It didn't take more than a few seconds after Lázaro's response, for those 3 soldiers to jump onto the yacht, and take everything that was in it out of its hold. Observing such efficiency caused Luis to comment to Lázaro in a low voice:

- I just saw in a pirate movie, how a ship is looted.

- Yes partner, live and direct - Lázaro replied.

- Now I do believe that this is authorized at the highest level of government in Cuba - Luis commented.

Lázaro and Luis boarded the Cuban ship and were taken to a place on the coast where there were several civilians fishing, including a child. There, the blue Land Rover was waiting for them, which they boarded together with Sánchez Lima and Juan Carlos, an army captain who came with them.

Already in the vehicle, Lázaro commented to Luis in a low voice:

- You saw how the civilians disappeared when these people arrived.

Indeed, the civilians who were fishing, as soon as they saw the boat and the Land Rover arrive, went up in smoke.

- Under dictatorships, things work like this - Luis replied.

The Land Rover started at full speed. They crossed the most famous tourist center of Cuba, the beach of Varadero. They passed by the Airport, the place through which many Cubans had left the country, on the Liberty Bridge. Later through Camarioca, also the place of departure from Cuba to the United States. In boats, they arrived at the Peñas Altas junction and ran along the Central highway towards the Athens of Cuba, the city of rivers, the once cheerful Matanzas.

The panorama was one of total calamity, the streets full of potholes, the buildings faded in the best of cases and destroyed in the worst, poorly dressed passers-by ran like crazy always with a bag under their arm.

Lázaro felt sorry for those poor people. The hatred that he felt before, for a people that had hurt, imprisoned and mistreated him, disappeared.
"Sometimes hate turns into pity," he thought to himself.

They crossed Matanzas at lightning speed and entered the Via Blanca, a highway that runs parallel to the sea, from Matanzas to the City of Havana.

Lázaro always in a low voice commented to Luis:

- This road was built under the government of Doctor Ramón Grau San Martín.

- And who was Ramón Grau? Louis asked him.

- The founder of the Authentic Party, a very intelligent man and former president of Republican Cuba.

The Land Rover, avoiding the potholes in the road, crossed the Bacunayagua Bridge, to the right the Punta de Ruvalcaba, and to the left the beautiful Yumuri valley, national pride, Santa Cruz del Norte, the beaches of Santa María and Guanabo.

At the roundabout they left the Vía Blanca and took the Monumental which took them to the tunnel that a French company had built to join the exit to the bay. They crossed the tunnel and took the Havana boardwalk.

The Land Rover raced west along the boardwalk. They passed the tunnel under the Almendares River and entered Fifth Avenue to the Marina Barlovento where, at the Hotel Ernest Hemingway, Raulito and the Moto were waiting for them.

They arrived and Luis and Lázaro were taken to the top floor of the hotel. A surprise awaited Lázaro that would tear down one of the great lies of castro communism, the lie of having eradicated prostitution.

As the old saying goes tell me what you boast and I'll tell you what you lack.

In the hotel room, Raulito and Moto were not alone. They were accompanied by a group of beautiful girls.

Moto called one of them and told Lázaro:

-Look, Julito, this girl's name is Carmen and she studied history like you. She is going to be your bodyguard in Cuba.- she said sarcastically.

Lázaro did not fully understand what was happening and looked from head to foot at that girl who was the living image of the flower in misery. She was dressed in cheap terry cloth and old sandals.

"Yes, brother, she's going with you," Moto told Lázaro, winking at him.

The girl took his hand and since Lázaro wasn't Pinocchio either, she let herself be carried away by that beautiful current.

Moto took the floor again:

- Luis and you are now going to a house that we rent in Villa los Cocos on the beach of Santa María del Mar. We are going there tomorrow.

- Well, if things are like this, let's go, I'm very tired - Lázaro replied.

Carmen Cecilia (PHOTO) was a beautiful 30-year-old Cuban, with a statuesque body that attracted a lot of attention among men. Single and childless, she had a little sister, Mercedes, who was her greatest adoration. Born to a Mexican father and a Cuban mother, both separated when she was a teenager. A short time later, her father returned to Mexico, leaving the family without any financial support. When she was 25 years old, Carmen had an affair with a man much older than her, who promised to get her out of the country. In the end, her dream went up in smoke, when her former partner was expelled by the Cuban government.

Lázaro knew perfectly well that most young Cuban women dream of emigrating to the civilized world and he had no doubt that this beautiful girl next to him was no exception. What he never imagined is that 7 years later they would meet again for something much more transcendental than what they were going to do that night. That story, later.

Already on the way with Captain Juan Carlos at the helm of the Land Rover, Carmen told Lázaro:

- I want to stop by my house.

- Stop by your house for what? Lázaro asked.

- To pick up clothes - Carmen answered.

- Where does the lady live?

- I live in the Luyanó neighborhood, on Fábrica street.

- In what street? - Lázaro asked - In Fábrica and Municipio, Fábrica and Arango, and Rodríguez, and Pérez, and Santa Felicia, and Santa Ana, and Compromiso, and Herrera, and Calzada, and Mangos, and Remedio, and Quiroga, and Tres Palacios or Fábrica and Colina?

Carmen's mouth dropped open, Lázaro had told her all the streets on the corner of Fábrica.

- How long has it been since you left Cuba? asked the girl without getting out of her astonishment.

- That doesn't matter, what matters is that I'm from here and I have a good memory. Lázaro said proudly. Carmen did not know that she was facing a man with more data in her head than a Sopena dictionary.

"Good, no, very good," Carmen told him, smiling with admiration, evident for the first time on her face.

The Land Rover parked in front of the house number 90 of Villas los Cocos on the beach of Santa María del Mar. The house had 4 rooms, 2 on the ground floor and two on the upper floor. Lázaro and Luis would occupy the rooms on the upper floor.

Once inside the room, Lázaro and Carmen sat on the bed.

- Do you know why you are here? - Lázaro asked Carmen with a tone between excited and modest.

Lázaro has always been a man who valued the conquest of women more than the simple sexual act. He caused her emotion and excitement throughout the process of falling in love, of getting positive reactions. He always had the philosophy that it is better to buy his crush a $50,000 diamond ring than to pay a prostitute $50 for a moment of pleasure.

But at that moment everything was different. He had returned to his native Cuba under very special circumstances and had realized that Carmen was not there with him for pleasure, but because, surely, she was being blackmailed by government officials to comply. Her escort role must be in exchange for something that was important to her. There was even the possibility that she had been recruited to extract and report information on the new arrivals.

Before 48 hours were up, she would realize that she was right.

- Do you know? - Lázaro insisted.

The girl bowed her head sadly, and that had a tender effect on Lázaro, who couldn't help but be a romantic. At that moment he considered that it was necessary to make things very clear and with a relaxed attitude, he took the floor:

- Look miss, I'm up to date on matters of love. I have my relationship in Miami. I also have a mother, sister, and daughters and my duty as a man is to behave decently. If you don't agree, I'll buy you some presents tomorrow morning, call a taxi, go home, and we'll stay as good friends.

Carmen with her head lowered told him:

- Yes I agree. Perhaps the consequences of that abrupt departure were too severe.

- Well, if you want, I want too - Lázaro told him.

Carmen stood up on the bed and the towel dress that barely covered her body stopped fulfilling her function. She fell at her feet. Her silky white skin was briefly interrupted by two small breasts, but capable of knocking a Boeing 747 out of the sky. At least that's what the lucky witness thought of her. From there downwards curves worthy of a Renaissance painter were born, who had dipped her brush in a magic potion created to drive any mortal crazy.

Lázaro, from that moment on, completely forgot that he had not slept for two days in a row. On the contrary, he felt as if she had been born again.

Briefly it occurred to his romantic mind that this woman was not a novice when it came to sex, but the idea was completely dispelled when Carmen got down on her knees and began to undress him.

The next morning Lázaro woke up to a revelation, upset that he hadn't thought of it before. He had to take care of her mouth but not from the kisses of that generous young woman in bed but from the microphones that could be installed in his room.

It was already noon and the two of them were hungry as castaways. Carmen tried to speak and Lázaro, putting a finger over her mouth, told her not to say anything. The girl understood and obeyed. They left the house holding hands like two boyfriends, a good night of sex was enough for them to gain some confidence. They went to lunch, almost in silence, and then went down to walk along the beach.

- You wanted to tell me something in the room and I guess what you want to talk to me - Lázaro told Carmen.

- No, forget it, it's nothing important - she replied.

Lázaro took her hand and kissed it as a sign of respect and said:

- I sense that you want to say something, but why are you afraid? It is normal in a country where no one can be trusted. Speak, I am with them, but I am not one of them. I want you to tell me your story, but don't lie to me, tell me the truth.

Carmen looked into Lázaro's eyes searching for the truth, because a small mistake could cost her dearly. She finally decided to risk it.

-Your friend, he did not deceive you when he told you that I studied history. I was at university until the fourth year of my Bachelor's degree in History, but finishing the fourth year, I met a foreigner, a Chilean, an older man who was twice my age, but in spite of everything, I grew very fond of him. In the end, I felt very good with him. I think he fell in love with me. He changed my life, he gave me gifts, he gave me money, and he promised to take me with him to Chile. But one day, I think that in order not to have to pay him something, they declared him persona non grata, and expelled him from the country, they arrested me.

Lázaro interrupted Carmen with a question:

- But why you, what had you done?

Carmen tried a shy smile, reflecting great sadness, and she continued her story.

- They accused me of prostitution and took me to the Manto Negro prison.

- And there they went to recruit you? - Lázaro asked him with wide eyes of astonishment.

Carmen lowered her head again in a sign of regret and said:

- What else could I do, if I refused, I had to stay in that hell, starving and surrounded by lesbians.

Lázaro resumed the word, after swallowing a bit of uncomfortable saliva:

- And what do you really want to do now?

Carmen didn't have to think about the answer, and she told him:

- What the majority of the people want is to leave this island, even if it is for Yuma.

- I'm going to trust you, and I don't know how, but I'm going to try to help you.

- But it can't be legal, legally they're never going to let me out of here - Carmen told him, already risking everything.

- Now it can't be, let me get to Miami. - Lázaro promised, almost as a commitment.

-I know of a young woman who came to pick her up in a boat, I have saved money, I can pay.

Lázaro understood Carmen's desperate state and told her:

- I'm not going to forget about you, let me get to Miami and there I'll see what I can do for you, but now we're going back.

- Why don't you buy me a music cassette? -said the young woman, already returning to her own reality.

- And where can we buy it? - Lázaro asked.

- In the store of the Mar Azul hotel - the girl told him.

They walked to the hotel and entered a small store.

- Partner, this is the dollar area - an employee said aggressively.

- Yes, with dollars we are going to pay - Lázaro replied.

- Do you have ID, "compañero"? - the impolite employee asked again, using a very comunist term, which means "partner" in english. She certainly wouldn't use that tone if a couple of Yankees visited her store.

Lázaro with a smile asked him:

- Are you a sailor? -

- No, I'm not a sailor - replied the employee, visibly upset.

- If she's not a sailor, we're not partners, yes I have identification, ma'am - Lázaro replied, pronouncing the word ma'am with force.

The couple approached the counter and Lázaro showed him his Florida driver's license.

- We want a music cassette by Juan Manuel Serrat, the one brought by Pueblo Blanco.

The employee, now less confused, placed the cassette that Carmen had asked for on the counter and said:

- It's 5 dollars.

- How expensive - Carmen protested.

- Thank God we have the 5 dollars - Lázaro told him.

That employee asked him in a contemptuous and mocking way:

- Do you believe in God? I believe in the revolution.

Lázaro smiled and replied:

- Of course I believe, how can I not believe, look at what the bill with which I am paying you says.

- And what does the ticket say? Carmen asked him.

-IN GOD WE TRUST- answered Lázaro raising the 5 dollars in front of his face, making sure that the employee also sees it.

- And what does that mean? - she asked rudely.

"That we trust in God," Lázaro replied as he turned to leave the store, imagining the disgusted face on the revolutionary woman's face.

Lázaro once again felt sorry for the Cuban woman who was left behind, locked up in that fictitious world, with false ideas and lacking freedom. She perfectly represented a people hypnotized by the lies of a government that always controlled their minds, with the simple purpose of staying in power.

By then, in 1988, the failed experiment that was called the "Cuban Revolution" had failed miserably for almost 30 years, leaving behind a poor, ignorant people with no future.

Precisely for this reason the "internationalists" (as Cuban officials called them in those days) were visiting his homeland. To help them survive.

They left the store on the first street of Santa María del Mar and hailed a taxi, boarded it, and in less than 10 minutes they were in front of house number 90.

- How much is the race? Lázaro asked.

- It's five pesos, - the taxi driver replied.

Lázaro went to pay him with five dollars, the somewhat scared man told him:

- That ticket can cost me 5 years in prison.

- And because? Lázaro asked.

"The dollar is penalized in the country," Carmen replied, taking the bill from Lázaro's hand and paying with a national bill.
If there was a diabolical symbol that represented the hatred that Fidel Castro's government had against the United States, it was the US dollar. The sole possession of a ticket, no matter the denomination, was reason to imprison a common citizen, for treason against the country. Ironically, the information that Lázaro came to provide to the Cuban military in those days was going to allow them to collect millions of what they hated so much.

Several days passed without much news, until one morning Lazaro opened the window of his room and observed the presence of several Russian-made Cuban military vehicles a few meters from the house where they were staying. He immediately thought that they had taken the wrong address and that they had come to look for him at the wrong house because in his mind the meeting he was waiting for was going to take place in some government building.

"Stay here, I'm coming," she told Carmen that she had stayed with him all those days keeping him company.

Going downstairs he realized that his friends had decided to sleep late that day or maybe in their beds they had enough reason not to get up. All was silent, except for the sounds of the engines that could be heard through the closed door.

From one house to the other there were only about 20 meters. As soon as Lazaro left and began to walk towards the soldiers who were guarding the door, he began to think:

- These Cubans are tin-faced, who exploit the people, who enslave them."

Lazaro had no idea who he was going to find in that house, no one had ever told him who the government representatives who would meet with him were. When he got close to the vehicles parked in front of house number 84, he realized that he wasn't going anywhere. The guards motioned for him to enter through the door and up the stairs to the second floor. Due to the amount of security it was evident that inside that room there was someone of a very high rank, he even thought: "and is it not Fidel himself?"

The idea dissipated when the officer who was waiting for him upstairs opened the door for him and saw two men he had known for a long time. Neither was bearded and smoked cigars. They were very high-ranking officials of the Cuban government: one, General Jose Abrahantes Fernandez, Minister of the Interior, former bodyguard and personal friend of the Commander in Chief, Fidel Castro. One of the best known faces of the revolution at that time, who since 1985 had been in charge of one of the most important government ministries. He was one of the main people responsible for the creation of the MC, the division of the ministry that was in charge of the difficult mission of circumventing the US embargo and generating money to keep the Cuban economy afloat.

The second participant in the meeting was Colonel Antonio "Tony" de la Guardia, head of the MC.

- Excuse me - Lazaro said with some timidity and still surprised by such a surprise.

- Go ahead, my friend, please approach the table - said Abrahantes, extending his right hand to greet him.

"Nice to meet you," Lazaro replied, and after greeting the general he approached De la Guardia to shake his hand as well.

He thought about praising them for their fame and career but then he remembered who they really were and what he was feeling at that moment was simply awe, and not admiration.

On the table was a sea chart from Cuba. Lazaro immediately recognized the area he had in mind for his explanation. What these two soldiers wanted to know was where would be the best place to drop drug packages into the water from Colombian planes coming from the Cali Cartel. He had already explained to Lazaro in Miami days before that the Cuban military responsible for drug trafficking to the Florida coast was looking for alternative ways to prevent planes from having to land on military runways. This meant unloading the merchandise and taking the drug to the coast to deliver it to the speedboats that would make the 90 miles to the United States.

Very complicated.

The ideal was to launch the packages from the heights into the water and leave them there until the boats came to pick them up. There were always Cuban soldiers from the coast guard guarding the valuable cargo.

This operation left a lot of money for the Castro government, and in an easy way. They would not even have to touch the drug, they would only facilitate quick and close access to Colombian drug traffickers who would take care of all the steps of the process: loading the planes in Colombia, transporting them the 1,900 kilometers that separate Colombia from the Cuban coast and then distribute it in the United States through their already established networks.

In the event that someone discovers the origin of the boats loaded with narcotics, the Cuban government would simply deny its intervention, alleging that everything was done illegally using its territory. In fact, this happened on several occasions, culminating in 2 completely false summary trials that cost the life of Colonel Antonio de la Guardia, the same one who was there meeting with Lazaro, General Arnaldo Ochoa, a Cuban military hero, and two of his assistants, Major Amado Padron and Captain Jorge Martinez. The four were shot by order of Fidel Castro in July 1989.

The purpose of this farce mounted by the Cuban government was to demonstrate that there were no drug traffickers in that country and that this was what happened to those who dared to disobey the "high revolutionary morality" of the people.

Months after Ochoa and the Guardia were shot, General Abrahantes was removed from office and indicted on similar charges, including charges of embezzlement of government funds. He was sentenced to 20 years in prison but in 1991, just 2 years after entering prison, he was found dead in his cell, supposedly due to cardiac arrest. Lazaro says that he was murdered. They stopped giving him the high blood pressure pills he was taking, which caused his death.

- Here is the Bay of Cadiz, this is the ideal place to launch cargo - said Lazaro, pointing to an area to the east of Cayos Falcones, on the north coast of the island. - Here is the north of Matanzas, here is the entrance to Icacos, the bay of Cardenas, you cannot work here because there are many shallows. But in this one, in the Bay of Cadiz we can throw away and there we pick up.

Author's note: The Bay of Cadiz now has another name. It is called Bahía de Santa Clara and it is located between Cayo de las Cinco Leguas and the city of La Teja. In that place there is a detachment of the Cuban Border Guard patrol, which had the task of monitoring the shipments that the planes dropped into the water.

And after a brief pause that he made on purpose to see if there were any questions, he added: - In this place the packages are going to keep floating near the coast and not the tide is not going to take them out to sea, even if they take time to pick them up.

Abrahantes looked at the map in silence. De la Guardia took the floor.

- And the fast boats will not have a problem with the depth in that area?

- No, - answered Lazaro quickly - there are all the ideal conditions for what you want. Good depth, discretion, security of cargo, out of sight of the yankee coast guards, and easy to find, because there is the lighthouse which is a good visual reference point for both planes and boatmen.

Abrantes finally, perhaps out of courtesy or to avoid losing face with Lazaro, decided to speak.

- How is it that you are so expert in maritime charts of Cuba, have you made many trips here?

Lazaro suspected a double meaning in his question and decided to go the simplest way.

- I know these waters very well, however I have never worked for you. When I was notified of this internationalist meeting, I decided to study well all the options for the mission that had been assigned to me, - Lazaro said, trying to sound as professional as possible - and that is why I came to this conclusion.

Abrantes looked at him curiously, his unfriendly face changed to a military one, suspicious and a little somber.

- So you're not a drug dealer? he asked with authority.

"I'm a smuggler," Lazaro clarified with an answer that he had already prepared beforehand. - there is a big difference. - I move what they ask me, what gives me money. They can be drugs, and only marijuana - he clarified firmly - gold, diamonds or works of art - he finished saying with a bit of sarcasm.

What Lazaro would never say in that room full of soldiers is that on several occasions he had smuggled humans, helping relatives, friends and strangers to escape from the repressive hell that is Cuba.

- Mostly I work for Colombians through the Bahamas and some shipments coming from Jamaica. But this is my first foray into Cuban waters to deal with issues related to the movement of drugs. - adds Lazaro, making it clear that he was not entering someone else's territory without permission.

"I'm not accusing you of anything, my friend," said Abrantes, understanding the weight of his words and, perhaps, preventing that advantageous relationship for his plans from being ruined as soon as it began. - I only ask you because we want to keep in touch with you for other situations like this, when we need information about delivery points.

- I am not offended, General, I just want to make it clear that I do not interfere with Cuba without having the authorization of the commander in chief, I know what he is capable of doing to people. - Lazaro replied and then regretted having brought up the subject.

- The commander is not going to be angry. - The Colonel
of the Guard interrupted, sensing a bit of tension in the
environment. - Here we are all working for the same goal,
for the good of the revolution.

Lazaro opted for silence. The three bullet wounds he had
on his body hurt a little bit. He knew that if he opened his
mouth that meeting could end very badly and that it would
be very difficult to collect fees from him if he did.

-That seems very good to me, each one takes care of what
he loves, right? he replied, surprised by his diplomatic
ability.

- Any other place you recommend? - asked De la Guardia?

- For what you need, no. All the others are from the south
side of the island and it would add many miles to the trip of
the boatmen or you would have to transport the packages
across the island. I did not find it practical to recommend
other places. I know that in this business you have to be
practical and fast, the more efficient the better.

Lazaro was giving a lesson in marine cartography and felt
that he was validating his bachelor's degree in history. He
immediately noticed that the faces of the two Cuban
soldiers seemed to indicate that they had run out of
questions and that the meeting was over.

- Thank you very much, - both soldiers said almost in
unison, as they took the map from the table to roll it up.

One of the escorts approached Lazaro and touched his
arm, a universal sign that we must find the exit.

"Nice to meet you," Lázaro lied, who at that point in the meeting had recalled in more detail the atrocities perpetrated by the Cuban regime on all his people, including his family, which was almost dissolved at the beginning of the revolution. Seven of his cousins were shot by Castro's troops. He recalled his time as "planted" in Cuban prisons, when he refused to dress like common prisoners because he was, along with many others, a political prisoner of conscience. And not to mention the anguish that he experienced hearing the cries of torture or the sound of rifles during the executions that he heard when he was imprisoned in his youth.

- At least Carmen is going to take everything from me, all this stress, - he thought to himself as he went down the stairs, leaving behind the murmur of those men who now knew how to smuggle more and better Colombian marijuana into the United States.

It is important to clarify that both the relatives of General Abrantes, his children and a nephew contacted for this book, as well as Ileana, the daughter of the Colonel of the Guard who lives in France, flatly deny the existence of this meeting. They maintain that the two soldiers never participated in drug trafficking activities and that the accusations that emerged a few months after this meeting with Lazaro were invented by the government of Fidel Castro to clean up its image internationally.

Ileana de la Guardia clarified: - In addition to the fact that my father never participated in these illicit activities, it seems impossible to me to think that two military officers of such a high rank inside were going to meet with a complete stranger, who could perfectly be an undercover agent of the North American government, to talk about such sensitive issues. -

A couple of nights after the meeting with Abrahantes, Lázaro called Miami to talk to Rosa, her favorite friend, and she gave him devastating news.

- Papi, Motico died - Motico was Armando's youngest son, el Moto, only 2 years old.

His friend and fellow smuggler was in the room below, with their respective Cuban friend, completely oblivious to the tragic news..

- But how did that misfortune happen with a child of only two years of age? Lázaro asked, feeling his soul sink to the ground.

-Liberty, the mother, she fell asleep, it could be that she was drugged, the child fell into the pool, and drowned. - Rosa cried silently on the other end of the phone.

- But are you sure of what you say? Lázaro asked, still not believing what he was hearing.

Motito was a beautiful little boy, his father adored him. He bore his name, Armando.

- Of course daddy, today we are going to watch over him.

- Well that's fine, tomorrow I'll call you again - Lázaro said to Rosa and hung up.

- What happened? Carmen asked him.

- Apparently in Miami Moto's youngest son died, but we won't tell him until tomorrow. Let's let him rest today. Tomorrow I'll see how I break the news. -

But Lázaro had forgotten that Carmen was Mercedita's sister, Moto's partner, and the news leaked, and in the morning the matter created a crisis.

- We have to talk - Luis told Lázaro, while they had lunch.

- I know that it is not in the original plan, because you only came as an advisor, to teach these people how to pick up water, because I have worked with brave people, but I do not work with suicides, and the mental situation of the Moto , is now, that of a suicide.

- And what do you want to do? Lázaro asked.

- That has no mystery partner, I want you to come with me.

- That also changes my payment - Lázaro replied.

- And how much do you think is fair? Because the distance is short - assured Luis with a complacent tone.

- You know that the greatest danger is in the last 20 miles, where all the enemies are together, the coast guard, the Customs service, the Florida Marine Patrol, Marine Fauna and Flora, and local police, plus the tumblers who want to rob you .

- Okay, I understand you, tell me, how much do you want to earn? Louis asked him.

Lázaro's response was clear and direct:

- The kilo at this moment is $2,000, I want $500 per piece.

- We are talking about 250 thousand dollars - said Luis.

- Take it or leave it friend, that's fair, I'm risking 30 years of life, that's fair, the good life is expensive, there is cheaper, but it's not life - was Lázaro's response.

- Okay, I agree - was Luis's answer.

Lázaro resumed the word.

- Call Colombia and tell them to put a GPS on the plane, to tie down the packages of five and to put lights on it, because we are going to pick up late in the afternoon, if the sea is a little rough, it can catch us at night.

- Do you want to pick up in Bahía de Cádiz? Louis asked him.

- No, we are going to pick up this time north of the Nono Grande Lighthouse, about two or three miles out to sea - was Lázaro's response.

- So close to shore?

- Does the operation have the authorization of the highest level? - Lázaro asked with a gesture of surprise.

- Well, that's what they told us and I think so - answered Luis.

- So what's the problem, follow me, I know the way, I know how to pick up water and skinny women.

- I'm going to call Colombia to give the green light to Operation Penguin - Luis said relieved. You don't play with the Cali cartel, much less being in Cuban territory.

- Don't forget about the GPS and the lights, so that we don't lose any packages, each one worth 400 lucas. - Lazaro said as they parted ways.

Several days of tension, boredom and enjoyment passed, each one in his world, but like everything that is expected comes one day, one afternoon Luis called Lázaro and told him:

- Start saying goodbye to your girl, we'll work tomorrow. -

- Okay, tonight I'm going to throw the rest with her, because you never know when the bull is going to hook you, you never know when you're going to lose, and remember what the deal is: I'll take a package as soon as possible. Soon we arrive at the Florida Keys, I'll take it under my arm, like a thermometer - Lázaro finished by saying.

At two in the afternoon of the following day, with Juan Carlos at the helm, Major Sánchez Lima at his side and Luis and Lázaro in the back seat, the Land Rover set out on its way to Varadero beach, according to the Cubans, the beach most beautiful in the world. They arrived around

5 PM, and went to a dock where they boarded a 36-foot Mirage, with two powerful 250 HP Mercury engines, guided by the Formula of the Cuban border guards.

Once in the open sea, the Cuban boat returned to the coast, and they put themselves in the planned place, about 4 miles north of the Mono Grande Lighthouse, Luis sat in front of the rudder and put the radius of two meters on the console, Lázaro took a seat next to the engines.

It would be a little after 6 in the afternoon, when they heard the voice of the captain of the plane say:

- Captain, this is Penguin.

Luis with the speed of lightning took the radio and answered:

- Penguin, this is Master in position, I'm going to give you the longitude and latitude of our GPS position.

- Captain, I don't have a GPS, I'm flying on radials.

Luis immediately turned to Lázaro and said:

- The plane is flying by radio, the captain says that it does not have a GPS, how is it going to find us?

- That's why I chose this place, I know a lot about this and skinny women. - Lazaro said with irony but also pride, another smuggler would have had a panic attack.

- I know that you know a lot about skinny women, but tell me what we are going to do now.

Luis was trying to joke around to hide his nerves. If they lose this shipment or lose face with Colombian drug traffickers, the consequences could be catastrophic.

- Don't worry, partner, the team wins. Tell the pilot to look for a lighthouse that is on the tip of the peninsula.

Luis told the pilot what Lázaro had said.

- Captain, I'm already seeing the lighthouse - answered the pilot.

Lázaro took the radio and said:

- Pass over the lighthouse and head north, frankly, and there you will see us.

Ten minutes later, a yellow air commando, with a penguin drawn on its tail, passed low over them.

- Start throwing the packages, flying in circles - ordered Lázaro.

Before the astonished gaze of tourists and nationals who were enjoying the beach before sunset, packages began to fall from the plane onto the waves.

One, two, three, all separated crashing loudly into the water. They had not been tied down as Lazaro had requested, nor did they have lights. In the distance a Cuban military ship could be seen at anchor, watching the spectacle. Accomplice. It never moved.

It took Lázaro and Luis more than an hour to get the packages out of the water and place them on the bow of the boat. This operation takes at least 3 men, with calm seas. There were only two of them and the sea had choked, but ambition for money sometimes makes a man double his strength. By nightfall they had finished collecting the 25 packages. The yellow air commando, now nicknamed "the penguin", had already left for Colombia.

From the beach they still watched the unusual spectacle, as if it were an episode of "Miami Vice". Perhaps some incredulous came to think that it was a humanitarian mission delivering food and medicine to the desperate Cuban people. It was not a bad idea, especially seeing the Cuban military patrol witnessing the process.

The original plan was to pick up the cargo and head straight for the Florida Keys, Lazaro's favorite place to get to the coast undetected. But due to the bad weather and the height of the waves, they had used more gasoline than estimated, and had to fill up the tank or risk being stranded halfway.

- Call on the radio and tell Sánchez that we have to go in to get gas. -

Half an hour later, the boat was moored at the pier of the Varadero Border Base. Night had already come and while they were taking the boat to fill the tank, Luis and Lázaro were sitting on the dock and they talked:

- This plane is slow and has flown over Cuba first from south to north and then from north to south, it is impossible for it to escape radar, it really is well authorized at the highest level - Luis told him.

Let's remember that this happened before the meeting with Abrantes and de la Guardia and neither of the two friends even knew the size of the drug trafficking network in Cuba.

- We have collected the 25 packages in front of everyone who was on the beach, they must have thought they were watching a movie - commented Lázaro.

One hour shortly after, the boat arrived at the pier captained by Colonel Blanco, the head of the Matanzas frontiersmen.

- Well partner, on horseback, what we came for - Luis told Lázaro.

"No, we're leaving at dawn, today we're going to change the rules of the game," Lázaro said to his companion.

- You're the captain, you're in charge - Luis replied.

The two of them lay down to sleep with the life jacket as a pillow on the cold, hard cement of the pier. At 5 in the morning they started the engines and headed out to sea for the Florida Keys.

- Put north, we are going to enter through Fiesta Key at noon, which is the time that the monkey put the monkey on the ground and told her to walk - Lázaro told Luis.

- By Fiesta Key at noon, won't that be too dangerous? Louis commented.

- Look partner, when it's not your turn, even if you put on, and when it's your turn, even if you take it off, I have a hunch that we're going to put this load out there today.

A few miles from the keys, they saw the coast guard passing by to the east, heading south, and Lázaro commented:

- Look where the tie goes, it goes to the Cayo Sal bank; That's how he catches us head-on. Don't stop here, not anymore, here you leave the job to customs or the Marine Patrol.

They got closer to land and Lázaro told Luis:

- Head for the 70 mile bridge, we're going to go under it.

They passed by the Tennessee lighthouse and noticed that next to the bridge, there was the Florida Marine Patrol boat.

- Stop an engine and lift it so that it believes that we have a broken engine. - Lazaro said nervously, sensing the danger lurking.

Luis obeyed immediately and as he passed by the boss, Lázaro greeted him with a sign of his hands. 15 minutes later, they were mooring at Fiesta Key. Operation Penguin was finished.

From the marina, Lázaro phoned Rosa and an hour later she picked him up with her package under her arm, as if it were a thermometer or a pan flute.

A pan flute valued at $400,000.

EPILOGUE

LIFE IS ONLY ONE AND YOU HAVE TO LIVE IT DANGEROUSLY

When in 1846 the Spanish poet Ramón de Campoamor wrote: "And in the treacherous world / there is nothing true or false: / everything depends on the color / of the glass through which one looks", he never imagined that, a century later, a little Cuban boy was going to build his life around those words.

Few people I know have defied life, and death, like that young Cuban who lay dying on a hospital bed, not knowing how much longer he would live. It can be said that he went through life on his own terms, in defiance of natural and divine law. In a world where many leave ephemeral marks along the way, where others must resign themselves to oblivion, he always found a way to resurface, to be reborn from the abyss.

Right or wrong, no one can say that Lazaro Garcia did not take risks, that he did not face life with courage. From the depths of a smelly cell, half naked and with little food, he reached the height of capitalism, he did it all. He was "planted" in a Cuban prison and became a millionaire. He was a prisoner without a future and also free as the wind.

He was everything he set out to be, and today, now in his seventies, he regrets nothing.

Lazaro Felipe Garcia Fonseca was born in Havana, Cuba on September 28, 1947 and at a very early age he realized, violently, that being in the wrong place, at the worst of times, is not a tragedy, it is just a circumstance of life . That pattern was to be repeated many times throughout his hectic existence. No longer with bullets, at least not in his body, but from decisions that led him to fulfill his dreams and, also, several times to jail.

Today, the wounds that he wears on his body are a mark of honor, a constant reminder that we are what we are and we must not fight against our own nature. For Lazaro, having reached the brink of death so young made him the man he is today, a lover of life, a philosopher adrift in a rough sea, who was always very clear about the course he should take.

When asked why he lived that way, he replies:

- Money… is what moves the world. Money can cause wars; prostitutes go to bed for money. Money, money, money… It corrupts and also makes many happy. But there comes a time when you have enough money to live on, ambition begins. And that brings vanity. Pablo Escobar was killed because he did not want to stop being Escobar. Chapo Guzmán was taken prisoner because he wanted to make a movie. " Lázaro reflects.

There are two types of men, those who tell the truth and those who live lying. Lazaro is one of the first. He never hid his ambition or his craft. "Zapatero a tus zapatos", if you want money, you have to go get it.

- Everyone in my family always knew what I did. And they told me "I love you very much and I admire you a lot". he says proudly.

As Machiavelli says, "the end justifies the means".

Why do you want to tell his story now? Good question.

During the decade he spent in prison, in his second stint in US justice, Lazaro dedicated himself to writing his memoirs. While others wasted their time playing dominoes outside his cells, he poured his life down on paper. Little by little, he created hundreds of handwritten sheets, full of memories, stories and fantasies from his mind. In the end, 20 books walked out of the prison with him.

Today, already a septuagenarian, he thinks that his life is worth telling. Although he has not yet fully accepted his obvious title of "drug trafficker" (he prefers to be called "smuggler" or "transporter"), Lazaro is proud of his journey through life and convinced that his story will inspire others to find their own. road.

The world is full of people who refuse to accept the reality of it, or who they are. Who live life making excuses to avoid the pain of the truth. That they blame their parents, their origins or the chicken feathers to justify their failures.

The story of this book, beyond its illegalities, tells the story of a man who did what he wanted, always understanding and accepting the consequences. If that's not bravery, then I don't know what to call it.

However, we cannot forget the historical aspect of his account. He is the only person who has presented irrefutable evidence of the involvement of the highest levels of the Cuban government in drug trafficking. Until now, no one, not even the US government itself with all its might, had put General Jose Abrahantes or Colonel Antonio de la Guardia in the same room, talking about the best routes to flood the United States with drugs.

Until now, no one told in great detail how the trips between Cuba or the Bahamas to the Florida coast were carried out. That is why this is a valuable historical document, which brings out the details of a world that is always hidden and mysterious, full of dangers and rarely told human stories.

Lazaro Garcia Fonseca is not a hero, much less a pillar of the community, however this does not detract from his story. His story deserves, without a doubt, a place in the planet's libraries, because it is unique and valuable, because his life is similar to that of many who do not have the courage to tell it. Because great inner peace and courage are required to open the floodgates of the soul and let everything come out without censorship, without remorse.

Campoamor said it clearly: "everything depends on the color of the glass through which it is viewed."

And the glass of Lázaro never clouded over.

www.ingramcontent.com/pod-product-compliance
Lightning Source LLC
Chambersburg PA
CBHW071930150726
47999CB00001B/168